The Vidas of
the Troubadours

The Vidas of
the Troubadours

Translated by
Margarita Egan

Volume 6

Series B

Garland Library of Medieval Literature

Routledge
Taylor & Francis Group

First published in 1984 by Garland Publishing, Inc.

This edition first published in 2018 by Routledge
2 Park Square, Milton Park, Abingdon, Oxon, OX14 4RN
and by Routledge
52 Vanderbilt Avenue, New York, NY 10017, USA

Routledge is an imprint of the Taylor & Francis Group, an informa business

Publisher's Note
The publisher has gone to great lengths to ensure the quality of this reprint but
points out that some imperfections in the original copies may be apparent.

Disclaimer
The publisher has made every effort to trace copyright holders and welcomes
correspondence from those they have been unable to contact.
A Library of Congress record exists under ISBN:

ISBN 13: 978-0-367-18943-3 (hbk)
ISBN 13: 978-0-367-18944-0 (pbk)
ISBN 13: 978-0-429-19943-1 (ebk)

The Garland Library
of Medieval Literature

General Editors
James J. Wilhelm, Rutgers Univesity
Lowry Nelson, Jr., Yale University

Literary Advisors
Ingeborg Glier, Yale University
Guy Mermier, University of Michigan
Fred C. Robinson, Yale University
Aldo Scaglione, University of North Carolina

Art Advisor
Elizabeth Parker McLachlan, Rutgers University

Music Advisor
Hendrik van der Werf, Eastman School of Music

The Vidas of
The Troubadours

translated by MARGARITA EGAN

Volume 6
Series B
GARLAND LIBRARY OF MEDIEVAL LITERATURE

Garland Publishing, Inc.
New York & London
1984

Library of Congress Cataloging in Publication Data
Vidas dels trobadors.
The Vidas of the troubadours.
(Garland library of medieval literature ; v. 6.
series B)
Translation of: Vidas dels trobadors.
Based on thesis (Ph.D.)—Yale University, 1976.
Bibliography: p.
Includes index.
1. Troubadours.   2. Poets, Provençal—Biography.
3. Provençal poetry—History and criticism.   I. Egan,
Margarita, 1948— . II. Series: Garland library of
medieval literature; v. 6.
PC3305.A34   1984   849'.13'09 [B]   83-20818
ISBN 0-8240-9437-9 (alk. paper)

Printed on acid-free, 250-year-life paper
Manufactured in the United States of America

The Garland Library of Medieval Literature

Preface of the General Editors

The Garland Library of Medieval Literature was established to make available to the general reader modern translations of texts in editions that conform to the highest academic standards. All of the translations are original, and were created especially for this series. The translations attempt to render the foreign works in a natural idiom that remains faithful to the originals.

The Library is divided into two sections: Series A, texts and translations; and Series B, translations alone. Those volumes containing texts have been prepared after consultation of the major previous editions and manuscripts. The aim in the editing has been to offer a reliable text with a minimum of editorial intervention. Significant variants accompany the original, and important problems are discussed in the textual notes. Volumes without texts contain translations based on the most scholarly texts available, which have been updated in terms of recent scholarship.

Most volumes contain Introductions with the following features: (1) a biography of the author or a discussion of the problem of authorship, with any pertinent historical or legendary information; (2) an objective discussion of the literary style of the original, emphasizing any individual features; (3) a consideration of sources for the work and its influence; and (4) a statement of the editorial policy for each edition and translation. There is also a Select Bibliography, which emphasizes recent criticism on the works. Critical citations are often accompanied by brief descriptions of their importance. Selective glossaries, indices, and footnotes are included where appropriate.

The Library covers a broad range of linguistic areas, including all of the major European languages. All of the important literary forms and genres are considered, sometimes in anthologies or selections.

The General Editors hope that these volumes will bring the general reader a closer awareness of a richly diversified area that has for too long been closed to everyone except those with precise academic training, an area that is well worth study and reflection.

James J. Wilhelm
Rutgers University

Lowry Nelson, Jr.
Yale University

TO BROOK, HAYDÉE AND FRED

Contents

Introduction

A noble and beautiful lady, a minstrel singing her praise, amorous intrigues and gossip in the castle of the wealthy feudal lords: such are typical elements of the world of the medieval love lyric which even today spark the imagination of writers and poets. Sources of these themes characteristic of troubadour love poetry can be traced to the princely circles of twelfth-century Southern France—the world of the Provençal poets. In later centuries, themes of troubadour love also appeared in prose, including the biographies of the troubadours, the *vidas* (lives), written in Old Provençal.

These texts, which have been little studied for their literary qualities, represent a vital link between the didactic tradition of the Middle Ages (commentaries, glosses on classical texts, exemplary lives of saints) and the fictional short stories of the Renaissance, such as the thirteenth-century collection of tales known as the *Novellino* and, later, Boccaccio's *Decameron*. Thus the vidas, the first literary biographies in a Romance tongue, can be examined as an important stage in the development of European narrative. At the same time these lively accounts allow modern readers to share the nostalgia and curiosity of the medieval audience about the poets of Provence (see Jeanroy, *Poésie lyrique*, I, 109–149; Favati, *Biografie*, pp. 11–109; Boutière-Schutz, *Biographies*, pp. viii–xlvii; complete details in Select Bibliography).

Authors and Texts

The *vidas* of the troubadours appear in the manuscripts as short introductions to and commentaries on the poets' lyrics. Some of the collections of troubadour poems—*chansonniers*—present vidas as prefaces to the verse selections. The earliest *chansonniers* with vidas date from the middle to the late thirteenth century. The first collection is generally placed between 1250 and 1280 (Avalle, *Let-*

teratura, p. 106; Favati, pp. 49, 65, 105; Boutière-Schutz, p. x). However, later evidence suggests that by the fourteenth century the vidas had achieved the status of an independent literary genre. Manuscripts from that period group them together, separated from the Provençal lyrics (Paris, Bibliothèque Nationale Fonds Français 22543 and 1749; Rome, Biblioteca Chigi, 1 iv 106). In any case, we do not know when the vidas were first composed, since the texts may have passed through several stages of formulation prior to their appearance in the first *chansonniers*.

The authorship of the vidas is generally uncertain, since only two of the 110 vidas are signed. Although most vidas are anonymous, it is widely assumed that they were composed by exiles from Provence living in Italy (Boutière, "Quelques observations," "Les italianismes," and "Les 3e personnes"). Beyond that assumption however, the literary and historical circumstances of their composition have hardly been examined. How and why were the vidas devised? For what audience? By contrast to our relative ignorance about the vidas, we are well informed about the authors and circumstances of the troubadour lyrics. The earliest poetry of Romance vernacular flourished in twelfth-century Provence, where, in noble halls, poets and *joglars* (minstrels) performed melodies and songs, usually expressing love themes. Their admiring audiences were ladies, lords, and courtiers, all with a taste for art, music, and polished poetry (Zumthor, pp. 466–75). But can the "lives" of the troubadours somehow be traced back to the same occasions and settings of the lyrics? How did the vidas come into existence, and do they bear any direct relationship to the poetry which they introduced in the manuscripts? Perhaps the best approach to these questions is to examine the texts of the vidas themselves. Then we shall consider this "internal evidence" in light of the literary and historical background of the later stages of the troubadour lyric, that is, the thirteenth century, the period of the first vida manuscripts.

Artistic Achievement: The Vidas as Stories

The charming and anecdotal vidas have lamentably remained on the fringes of scholarly interest ever since they were first perceived to be historically unreliable. Critics long ago dismissed them as fanciful and fictitious (see, most recently, Guida); scholars have failed to realize that, though the vidas contain much historically unattestable information, they nonetheless comprise an independent literary genre of some importance. General ignorance about these texts has been reinforced by the absence of a systematic examination of their content and structure which will here be sketched.

Two basic issues must be considered: how people and actions are described by the authors of the vidas, and what elements the texts have in common. Several terms used in the vidas to introduce poets, ladies, and patrons recur frequently. Words such as *savis*, *enseignat*, *cortes*, and *larcs* commonly appear in the vidas, where "learnedness, wisdom," (see Vidas 28, 41, 50, 75, 76, 97), "courtliness" (27, 38, 43, 46, 72, 97) and "generosity" (27, 93) are ideals of behavior and character. Predictably, good poets are always good wooers of ladies, who are themselves always described as *bellas* (beautiful). Among the few women in the vidas, only seven are poets: 8, 12, 23, 26, 63, 65, 96. Moreover, the poets are at ease among the nobility, and are well-schooled (see 6, 46, 56, 67, 72, 82). Also typical are troubadours who are versed in the active ideals of courtliness and who exhibit knightly talents: Bertran de Born, for example, is said to be very able in battle (17; see also 38, 91). Troubadours are almost always described as talented composers of music and verse, "subtle in words and in understanding" (4; also 14, 17, 36, 41, 59); some biographers, however, do not hesitate to criticize the quality of a poet's verses (28, 30, 32, 64, 77), or to tell of his lack of popularity (42, 87).

Interestingly, not only are the words similar which are used to present the individual characters of the poets, but the arrangement of the words is uniform as well. The terms that describe persons tend to occur in set patterns, in such a way that the name and place of origin of the protagonist, his social status, and his character nearly always appear in the same order. Sail d'Escola, his vida tells us, was from Bergerac, from a rich town in Périgord, the son of a merchant. He became a jongleur or minstrel and made good little songs (92). The biography of Bertran d'Alamanon describes its subject in a similarly formulaic way: Bertran, we are told, was from Provence, the son of Pons de Brugeiras; he was a courtly knight who was eloquent in speech (16; 14A and B, 37, 82, 101).

Characters of secondary importance in the poet's story (ladies, patrons, and others) are seldom described in detail. More often than not, they are only named, although in a few cases a description of the poet's profession or social status helps to portray them ("and he loved a burgher from Orlac, whose name was my lady Galiana," 45; see also 10, 11, 12, 29, 40, 82, 83).

Thus far, we can say that different vidas describe their subjects in surprisingly similar ways, and that certain patterns reappear throughout the corpus. Whether the vida is long or short, whether it concerns a celebrated or lesser troubadour, it typically portrays its subject in a formulaic way. The question we must now pose is: are these patterns part of larger and more complex patterns? Besides telling us similar things about who the troubadours were, do the "lives" also tell us similar things about what they did? Are the activities of different poets analogous to one another? Are there narrative patterns as well as descriptive ones in the troubadour biographies? How do such patterns relate to one another?

The themes of love and patronage occur in varying contexts throughout the vidas. Let us now examine how these themes are woven together into the "lives" and also what formal elements the different accounts of a troubadour's amorous and political adventures have in common. The simplest vidas appear as static portraits of the troubadours: they tell us something about the poet and the fact that he composed poetry. Sometimes the poet is described in detail; at other times we are told what types of poems he wrote and what sorts of melodies he devised. But in general these brief "portrait vidas" consist only of a sequence of qualifiers describing the poet's attributes and a short narrative sequence recounting his poetic composition (4, 12, 36, 38, 43, 47, 59, 61, 70, 85, 89). Although this basic scheme is changed occasionally, exceptions are rare (34, 36, 45, 70, 89, 95).

As an example, let us take the vida of Richart de Tarascon (No. 90):

> Richart de Tarascon was a knight from Provence, from the
> castle of Tarascon. He was a good knight and a good
> composer of poems and a good servant of ladies. And he
> composed good *sirventes* and good songs.

This account contains only two sequences: a descriptive sequence ("Richart . . . ladies") followed by a narrative sequence ("And . . . . good songs"). Similar is the structure of all brief vidas, which can be summarized by the following statements, each indicating a compositional unit:

      Poet is described
      Poet composed poems

It is clear that these simple "portrait vidas" are really no more than a joining of the basic descriptive structure with the briefest of narrative sequences. This biographical kernel provides the core of the increasingly complex narrative structures which comprise the longer vidas. As an example, let us turn to those vidas that we might call "portrait stories."

In this group of texts, wandering troubadours seek support and protection from wealthy nobles, and they meet with success or failure. Most such vidas tell of the poet being welcomed and accepted into the courtly milieu, given material riches, honor and praise (1, 22, 29, 33, 52, 66, 75, 80, 87, 101). Patronage stories underline the economic importance of courtly politics for the troubadour; without the support of a noble friend, the poet would be forced to abandon his craft. Only within the context of the court could he manage to survive. Therefore in those vidas whose subjects fail to secure patronage, for example, poets leave to join religious orders or wander from court to court and country to country in search of friends (33, 52).

Patronage stories generally consist of a descriptive sequence describing the poet and a narrative sequence recounting his relations with sponsors. Or, to state the elements schematically:

      Poet is described
      Poet composed songs
      Poet had patron
      Patron accepted poet

This model in itself becomes more complex as it is embellished in other patronage stories. Some poets, for example, react to a patron's rejection by taking action themselves. When they cease to be passive objects of another's wishes, the poet-protagonists subsequently affect the outcome of the plot. Rejected by patrons, these poets leave court, join monastic orders (abandon the secular world), or simply stop singing.

A schematic representation of these longer patronage stories might be summarized as follows:

      Poet is described
      Poet composed songs
      Poet had patron

> Patron rejected poet
> As a result, poet left secular world or poetry

Rejection and acceptance are also dominant motifs in the next group of vidas which we can characterize as love stories. By contrast to patronage stories, which tend to include at most one subject in addition to the poet, love stories usually have three or more. Here as before, other personages act, causing the poet to react. Typically the biography tells us that a troubadour loved a lady whose affection he desired. Love inspired his song. In the basic scheme, the lady reciprocates the poet's love. He composes lyrics exalting her and performs other worthy deeds in her honor (15, 37, 83, 84):

> Poet is described
> Poet loved lady
> Lady loved poet
> As a result, poet composed songs

Within certain love stories, a stable liaison will be ended by one of the lovers. Ladies sometimes enter nunneries (60, 86), abandon their lovers (76, 87, 91, 98), or die (29, 33, 58, 82). The poet-lover responds to these events by going away, taking the cross, or even going mad (29, 33, 58, 76, 82, 91, 92). When the poets die, their ladies take drastic steps or similar actions: Jaufre Rudel's lady becomes a nun, as does Raimon Jordan's (60, 86). Thus, once again, more complex love stories are built up from the basic unit seen in the simpler texts. In short, these longer love stories, in which the poet is rejected, can be schematized as follows:

> Poet is described
> Poet loved lady
> Lady loved poet
> As a result, poet composed songs
> Lady rejected poet
> As a result, poet left secular world or poetry;

or, in a different version (that in which the poet dies),

> Poet loved lady
> Lady loved poet
> As a result, poet composed songs
> Poet died
> As a result, lady left secular world

With the appearance of a third personage, the plots of love stories expand accordingly. Opponents of the lovers (usually the lady's husband or brother) either reassert control over her or kill the poet, and the poet-lover has no choice in the matter. If he survives, he must leave the lady and abandon his courtship (see 3, 14, 53, 79). To summarize, these stories tell us:

Poet loved lady
Lady loved poet
As a result, poet composed songs
Opponent rejected poet and lady
As a result, poet left lady

When a fourth personage intervenes to counteract the opponent's action, the poet wins his lady back (39, 68, 73) or simply abducts her (94). The structure of these stories can be described as follows:

Poet loved lady
Lady loved poet
As a result, poet composed songs
Opponent rejected poet and lady
As a result, poet separated from lady (or lady rejected poet)
Helper aided poet
As a result, poet and lady were reunited

Again and again in the vidas, we have seen that the protagonists remain essentially the same, as do, for the most part, their actions. But if so many patterns of form and content appear in the corpus, more difficult questions now confront us. Why do the vidas of more than one hundred troubadours resemble one another so much? What circumstances led different authors composing biographies of so many different poets to follow the same basic thematic and structural framework? How and why were they created?

Purpose of the Vidas: Lore and Learning

To approach the problem of the vidas' composition—who wrote them and for what reason—we must try to place the apparent patterns of form and content in a literary and historical context. Since most of our texts are anonymous, any discussion of origin and authorship must necessarily remain speculative, as has been the tradition of previous scholarship on these questions. Nonetheless, the foregoing formal analysis should provide a new and more helpful perspective. Let us begin by reviewing the kinds of information contained in the biographies.

Broadly speaking, the troubadour vidas provide information from two types of sources. First, there are certain biographical facts about the poets which can be shown to be derived from their poetry; for present purposes we may call such information "literary." Second, there is material from sources unconnected with the poet's own verses, which we may call "non-literary." In this latter case, the author of the vida provides facts drawn from witnesses to the life of the poet, such as his mistress, relatives, or acquaintances; the biographer may also have consulted written records about the poet, learned facts through hearsay, or simply invented some of the details in the troubadour "life."

Unfortunately, the biographical elements of the vidas cannot always be neatly assigned to "literary" or "non-literary" categories. Some of the material drawn from the poems may be historical (though unverifiable) and certain seemingly non-literary facts may have been drawn from poems now lost to us. Since much of the information in the vidas is not easily traced to any known source, we must acknowledge the possibility of stages or processes of composition which cannot be uncovered. Within such limits, however, we may profitably examine the literary and non-literary material in greater detail.

Links between a troubadour's verse and the prose vida written about him are easily demonstrated on linguistic and thematic levels. Love and patronage are typical themes of the vida stories; this, of course, can be said of many lyrics as well. We also note that those vidas which develop non-romantic themes center on poets who did not sing of love. The biography of Bertran de Born (17), for instance, speaks of his ability to foment discord between the kings of France and England, and of the poet's well-known songs and debates on the virtues of war. The vida of Marcabru also tells of the poet's relations with other men: how the troubadour was hated by local nobles for his acrimonious verses decrying the falsity and superficiality of their lives (64). It is not surprising that these two vidas neglect to speak of love and courtliness, patrons or erotic intrigues. The verses of Bertran de Born and Marcabru have little to do with ladies and courtship.

The debt of the vidas to the lyrics is even more obvious when we examine linguistic borrowings. Firstly, all of the standard terms which we have seen used to describe poets, ladies, and patrons in the vidas appear in similar descriptions in the lyrics. Thus, troubadours in their poems call themselves *cortes* (courtly); their patrons are addressed as *larcs* (generous), and their ladies are portrayed as *bellas* (beautiful).

In addition, vidas often explain specific metaphors and proper nouns found in the poems, ascribing biographical significance to them. The troubadour Jaufre Rudel, for instance, sang of an elusive *amor de lonh* (far-away love) who is otherwise unidentified. His biographer interprets the phrase by creating a tale of simple and evocative power: Jaufre loves an unseen lady and must travel to the distant city of Tripoli to see her (60). Thus Jaufre's faint images of far-away love are made concretely biographical and—the author of the vida must have hoped—comprehensible for his audience. Similarly, Arnaut Daniel's unusual metaphor of a hunter on an ox (*bou*) chasing a hare inspires the biographer to recount the poet's affair with a lady from Bouvilla, literally "Ox City" (10). Here the author of the vida even cites the relevant lines of the poem as historical evidence for what we know to be sheer fancy. Most vidas in the corpus have some biographical "fact" about the poet drawn from a specific part of his verse.

Indeed, many Old Provençal biographies are inspired by the reading of a poem. The authors of vidas incorporated in what they perceived to be a "historical" framework words and ideas derived from the lyrics. Moreover, when particular metaphors or proper names from the poems stirred the biographer's imagination, he did not hesitate to include them in his account of the poet's "life."

However, other elements of the vidas cannot be traced to the troubadour's poetry. When we have, for example, no linguistic or thematic evidence, either in the vida or in the troubadour's verse, to prove a link, we must consider the likelihood that the biographer made use of non-literary sources. Obvious examples of this kind of information include historical facts about the poet's birthplace, his social status, and his family background. Vidas occasionally include details about a troubadour's patrons, his beloved lady, or his religious persuasions—but in forms which suggest sources beyond the realm of the poet's own verse (Panvini, *Biografie*, pp. 17–18, 100–118).

How did the biographers of the vidas gain access to such information? The texts provide a few clues. Several vidas actually cite witnesses who reported directly to the author their personal knowledge about the poet. Raimbaut d'Aurenga's vida, for example, recounts how the poet's former mistress (later a nun) revealed the particulars of their romantic liaison (83). Uc de Saint Circ, composer of Bernart de Ventadorn's vida (14A), cites as his witness the poet's mistress' son:

> And I, Lord Uc de Saint Circ, have written down . . . what was told to me by the viscount Lord Ebles de Ventadorn, who was the son of the viscountess whom Lord Bernart loved.

Other vidas cite sources of information which are less specific, and in many cases less direct. The author of Cadenet's vida (22), for example, admits to having gathered information *"per auzir e per vezer"* (by listening and seeing). Whether this means that he saw and listened to the poet or people who knew the poet or to people who only knew about the poet, we cannot tell; he may also have consulted some kind of written records which contained facts about Cadenet's life. The biographer of Peire d'Alvernhe (67) records as a source the name of another person from the same region (and, in fact, the same period) as the poet, one Dalfin d'Alvernhe. But there is no clue whether the biographer spoke directly with Dalfin or merely borrowed his facts second-hand, through conversation or reading. Finally, many of the historical facts in the vidas are linked to no source at all and may have been merely incorporated from contemporary (but lost) legends and stories about the troubadours (Panvini, *Biografie*, pp. 121–139).

Whatever the sources of the biographers' historical facts, the reliability of their information varies. Much can be shown to be accurate through comparison with external historical materials (charters, wills, chronicles, and other documents) which still survive. Among the vidas providing information which can be verified by existing documents is that of Jaufre Rudel (60). Although based in large part on the poet's verse, this text contains several accurate details about his life. Jaufre is, for instance, called a "prince." Contemporary charters record that the lords of Blaye bore the title *princeps*, and thus we can safely assume that in real life our troubadour shared the title as well (see Panvini, *Biografie*, pp. 122–127; Cravayat). Other vidas with attestable historical details are that of Uc de Saint Circ (101), which gives precise topographical information about his birthplace; the "life" of Cadenet (22), which contains details of the poet's relations with patrons and other troubadours; and that of Folquet de Marseilla (33), which provides exact information about the controversial troubadour's retreat to the Abbey of Toronet (Stronski, *Folquet de Marseille*, pp. 87–90, 142).

But those same historical materials, as well as our modern common sense, will often demonstrate the opposite. The authors of the vidas sometimes make mistakes, ranging from the forgivable to the surprising. Guillem IX (Duke William IX of Aquitaine), for instance, is said by his biographer to have been the grandfather of Eleanor of Aquitaine (46). He was, in fact, her great-grandfather, as medieval documents testify. Cadenet's otherwise knowledgeable biographer (22) also makes some errors. He claims, for example, that the poet took on the pseudonym "Baguas." But this name, a masculine form of *bagassa* (prostitute), is not attested during Cadenet's lifetime (Appel, *Cadenet*, pp. 4, 94). Another imprecision, though minor, places Cadenet's home on the Durance River. The ruins of his castle are, in fact, several miles north of the river's shores.

Some "facts" of the vidas are neither accurate nor mistaken, but simply grew out of the authors' imaginations. Many are indistinguishable from historical facts whose sources are lost to us, but others are readily identifiable, and betray the authors' talents for invention. An obvious case of this kind of non-literary information about the troubadours is seen in the fabrication or explanation of proper names. The process is similar to the etymological glossing of words in the verses but differs in that the object of the gloss does not necessarily come out of the poems. In the vida of the early poet Cercamon (24), for example, the biographer gleans supposed facts merely on the basis of the poet's unusual name. "Cercamon," which we can see to derive from *cercar* (to search, wander) and *mon* (world), is supposed to have reflected the impoverished troubadour's itinerant existence: the biographer claims that Cercamon "wandered all over the world, wherever he could go, and for this reason had himself called Cercamon." Perplexing names thus become pretexts for elaborate explanations, in the same way that confusing metaphors in the poems inspire fanciful narrative episodes.

The multiple types of information in the vidas should warn us that the problems of their composition will not be easily solved. Furthermore, though patterns of form and content can be observed, there are enough variations among individual texts to suggest a less than uniform ancestry for the corpus. Nonetheless, it is worth pursuing the question of their origin and development in the light of what we have seen thus far.

Who composed vidas based on troubadour songs? The most obvious answer would be jongleurs or other troubadours. After all, they knew the poems well. It is not hard to imagine that a thirteenth-century troubadour or jongleur could recite at least a few poems composed by his mentors or simply by other well-known poets of earlier generations. Furthermore, many troubadours during the thirteenth century knew how to read and write (see 10, 29, 32, 41, 58); in fact, the two troubadours who are known to have composed vidas had been to school. They and other learned poets (a few others are attested) could have handled written as well as oral sources and applied their knowledge of troubadours to the composition of biographies, whether of predecessors or even contemporaries (see 101 and Panvini, *Le Biografie*, pp. 13–18; Lavaud, *Peire Cardenal*, pp. 608, 609, note 1).

The two vida texts with known authors provide a glimpse of the biographical process. In both the vida of Bernart de Ventadorn and that of Peire Cardenal, the respective composers, Uc de Saint Circ and Miquel de la Tor, take pains to identify themselves, and, in a sense, to sign their work. Each author points out to his readers or listeners the authenticity of his biography. Uc does so more explicitly by revealing that he spoke to a living witness (Ebles de Ventadorn) and one of the poet's descendants (14). For his part, Miquel lends credibility to his account by carefully documenting his own professional status (he is, he tells us, an *escrivan*, "writer") and by identifying Nîmes as the place where he composed his text (71).

Authorship of the remaining Provençal biographies can, by analogy to the examples cited, be attributed to other (though anonymous) troubadours and jongleurs. But there are, of course, other possible candidates. For instance, we know that scribes who transmitted manuscripts of troubadour songs certainly read the Provençal language and were thus also likely to write it. As they transcribed troubadour lyrics, copyists not only copied down but perhaps even invented some of the accompanying biographies.

The vidas sometimes appear in early manuscripts as rubrications (Manuscripts B [Paris, Bibliothèque Nationale Fonds Français 1592] and IK [Bibliothèque Nationale Fonds Français 854 and 12743]). They seem to have been devised as eye-catching prefaces for the poems. If so, we should speculate that scholars commissioned to compile anthologies of troubadour songs composed some of the vidas at the same time they were transcribing the verses. They needed little more, we know, than a mere clue to the troubadour's region of origin. With that and a poem or two to provide a few additional details, a scribe could easily have created a brief "life" to decorate his page of poetry.

The task of these thirteenth and fourteenth-century scribes differed little from that of contemporary commentators who collected and annotated classical Latin texts for use in schools. An interesting parallel exists, not coincidentally, between the Old Provençal vidas and other medieval commentaries and glosses prepared by clerics and scribes. Specifically because of their function as prefaces or introductions, the vidas resemble the Latin *vitae poetae*, part of the *accessus ad auctores*, introductions to twelfth and thirteenth-century glosses on Greek and Latin writers. The Latin *vitae*, like the Provençal vidas, draw supposed historical "facts" about the authors' lives from their writings: a corrupt line in an eclogue by Theodolus, for instance, led his medieval biographer and commentator to claim that the Latin author had died young, before he could correct his work (Huygens, *Accessus*, pp. 26–27).

Other resemblances between the *vitae poetae* and the Old Provençal biographies are remarkable: both speak of the poet's origins, of his social status, training, and travels; both describe the literary text which they introduce (Huygens, *Accessus*, pp. 1–17; Quain; Hunt). The *vitae poetae* are similar in content to the Old Provençal "lives." Like many of our vidas, the Latin texts speak of the poet's literary skills, of his origin and social position. The *vita* of the tenth-century poet Theodolus, for instance, first describes his education, then tells us about his travels and explains how his observations in various places affected his literary vision. The account, similar to numerous Old Provençal vidas, ends with a citation from Theodolus' poem.

Vidas and *vitae* also share analogous stylistic and thematic patterns: the *auctores*, like the troubadours in the vidas, perform only a limited number of actions, all relevant to the act of literary creation (they travel, study, observe). In the vidas, poets fall in love in order to compose poems; in the *accessus*, writers invariably convert to Christianity as a prelude to expounding their thoughts and experiences (Egan, "Commentary").

The similarities between vidas and *vitae* should not surprise us. Both works are, after all, literary biographies as well as prefaces, and it is probably significant that both vidas and *vitae* differ markedly from other biographical texts of the period. Saints' lives, for instance, dwell on the miraculous and exemplary aspects of their subject's existence, while biographies of political figures emphasize physical prowess and diplomatic skills (De Ghellinck, I, 62–64; Auerbach, pp. 156–168).

From this we can generalize that authors of vidas and *accessus*, both working primarily from poetic texts—though at different times and under different circumstances—composed remarkably similar "lives." The vidas stand in the tradition of these earlier medieval biographies, though direct influence cannot be demonstrated. There is, however, an important difference between the vidas and the *vitae poetae*. The structural parallels found in the two genres must not obscure the facts that the *accessus* were composed to be read silently and that they never directly addressed listeners. The vidas, by contrast, indicate (at least in some cases) that they were to be spoken or read aloud. Once we consider the question of audience, the actual circumstances of composition may become clearer.

We are aware that troubadour poetry flourished in a musical form, and that often songs were performed before they were written down. The vidas appear to have a similar oral tradition behind them. The phrasing of the "lives," for instance, is extraordinarily uneven and rough. Furthermore, unlikely syntactic constructions, and sentences and narrative units connected with *et* (and), *si* (indeed, yet), and *que* (that, whom) may well be the mark of improvisation before a live audience (Fernandez Pereiro; Ong, pp. 36–57; Schutz, "Where Were the Provençal *vidas* Written?" and "Were the *vidas* Recited?"). One can easily imagine, for instance, certain rambling passages being recited by a jongleur at court:

> And because of his wit and his inventiveness in poetry he gained great honor, so that the Dalfin of Auvergne took him as his knight and clothed him and armed him for a long time and gave him land and an income (80).

More obvious signs of oral performance also appear in the vidas. Though many texts end with a concluding statement such as "and here are written" (2, 32, 39, 71), some vidas announce the recitation of poems to follow: "as you will hear" (14). Occasionally in the course of his account, the biographer reminds his listeners of what they have heard: "as I have said" (15), or "as I have told you" (84). (For similar elements in the Old Provençal *razos*, see Egan, "The Old Provençal *vidas*," pp. 120–139.) In these cases we must assume that reading aloud or recitation of the troubadour verses followed what was an oral account of the troubadour's life. That account may have been originally composed "live," at the time of performance or written down ahead of time to be read aloud.

The earliest written vidas may have been embellished during performances. With the text of a troubadour biography before him, the jongleur could have provided further details extemporaneously, and from time to time, as he read, addressed his listeners directly. For example, when the jongleur announced to his audience that he would sing ("as you will hear"), he was inadvertently adding an oral aspect to the vida which he had before him in writing. In later written versions, the vida texts came to incorporate these various spoken elements.

In fact, some vidas actually preserve clues of combined written and oral origins. Bernart de Ventadorn's biography, for example, finishes by announcing that poems are about to be sung: "he composed these songs which you will hear . . . which are written below" (14A). The simultaneous reference to hearing and writing could perhaps signify that the performer was reading before a live audience. To help his memory he carried—as did other performers at the time—written versions of troubadour poems. But he may also have had abbreviated vida texts or biographical annotations that would have served to introduce his performance of troubadour lyrics (Chaytor, *Script to Print*, pp. 11–13; Schutz, "Were the *vidas* Recited?"; see also vidas 1, 2, 3, 14, 17, 23, 29, 39, 41, 60, 62, 68, 75, 80, 81, 82, 85, 86A, 86B).

Nonetheless, the question remains as to how the biographies became the written texts they are. It is possible that jongleurs devised the vidas orally during performances and eventually wrote them down in their working manuscripts. It is also possible that the biographies existed in brief written sketches and were embellished afterwards, first in the course of oral performances and later by the copyists of more costly songbook collections. A more detailed look at the historical context of the vidas may illuminate their earliest stages and the subsequent evolution of the texts as we have them today.

Survival and Perspective

The Albigensian Crusade (1209–1229) and the Inquisition that followed had important effects on the performance of troubadour poetry. First, the disruption of many Provençal courts drastically limited the patronage of the nobles, and composers and performers were forced to find new sponsors in neighboring Italy and Spain (Sumption, pp. 244–252; Anglade, *Troubadours*, pp. 172–195, 278–281; Camproux, pp. 60 ff.). Furthermore, in the wake of growing religious intolerance and the strictures instituted by the Dominicans newly arrived in Provence, secular poetry declined. The verse of thirteenth-century troubadours took on an increasingly moralistic tone, became didactic and religious in theme (see recently, Topsfield, *Troubadours*, pp. 241–252, 260).

Now in foreign courts the new patrons looked back admiringly to the more refined and vigorous songs of the twelfth-century poets, and the traveling jongleurs could offer their listeners the poems of a bygone age. Although the Old Provençal language was certainly understood by Spanish and Italian courtly audiences (Alvar, pp. 23 ff.), the names and places mentioned in troubadour poems and even their authors were, in all likelihood, unfamiliar. Thus younger troubadours and jongleurs may have devised the vidas to introduce, in live performance, these little-known songs from as long as one hundred years before and from a culture which no longer existed. Whether the vidas were first composed extemporaneously or prepared in advance to be read aloud can only be guessed. Some combination of the two is not unlikely.

The authors of these lively texts made the words and deeds of past poets understandable: they explained how the older troubadours searched for patronage, fell in love, and composed songs. The authors recounted the "lives" in Provençal, a language understood although no longer spoken by courtly Spanish, Italian, and French audiences. We might imagine that as the performer shifted from preface to poem, as he modulated his own voice to give life to another's words and melody, the greatness of the twelfth-century tradition lent dignity to the thirteenth-century man. The vida demonstrated its author's close link with the past.

The next most probable stage in the composition of vidas took place not in the court but rather in the libraries and *scriptoria*. Initially, the survival of troubadour poetry was assured by its continued performance in exile. However, by the mid-thirteenth century, devotees of secular poetry had begun to compile written collections of Old Provençal texts, probably including the introductory "lives" (see Marshall, p. lxxxii). Thus the vidas, together with lyrics, were set down as testimonies to a fading oral tradition. Thereafter, scholarship would promote another stage: once preserved in a static form, vidas became divorced from the poems they had formerly introduced. Now considered narratives in their own right, by the fourteenth century vidas were grouped together separately in the *chansonnier* collections.

Still later, following a number of transcriptions, the plots of many "lives" grew more complex. As scribes (or even other troubadours) continued to copy the texts of the vidas, dialogue was added to the stories and characters were further developed. The two versions of Guillem de Cabestaing's "life" provide a good example: the shorter thirteenth-century text (53A) is concise and direct, while the fourteenth-century version (53B) not only adds dialogue between the jealous husband and his unfaithful wife but also contains an elaborate epilogue describing the king's glorification of the lovers (see also 86A and 86B).

It is also quite likely that the same scribes and troubadours could have invented some new biographies as they copied down the lyrics; using information circulating in the courts, drawing on the poems and even their own imaginations, they might put together short "lives" to preface their selection of poetry, consciously or unconsciously following the model of previous authors of vidas. The corpus grew larger as it became a distinct genre; and it is as a genre that we may read and study the vidas today.

If the foregoing reconstruction is warranted, we must assume that the vidas passed through both oral and written stages. Because of that evolution from recited preface to literary biography, we can better appreciate the importance of the vidas in the development of the narrative tradition of the Middle Ages. As introductions to live performances of troubadour songs and as "pre-texts" to written poems, the Old Provençal "lives" represent a vital link between learned medieval commentaries in Latin and secular storytelling in the vernacular.

The vidas stand at the crossroads of various traditions. On the one hand, like medieval glosses, they look back to earlier works of "classic" poets and demonstrate—for the first time in the vernacular—the various assumptions held by medieval audiences about Provençal verse. On the other hand, as independent narratives, the vidas anticipate new and important literary forms: not only Dante's *Vita Nuova*, in which the poet offers prose explanations of his own verse, but also, perhaps more significantly, the *novelle* of the Italian Renaissance (see Dardano, pp. 1–45, 148–150; Neuschäfer; Egan, " 'Razo' and 'Novella' ").

The legacy of the vidas did not end with the Italian Renaissance. In the sixteenth century, Italian commentators turned to the Provençal "lives" in the course of their scholarship on Petrarch and Dante. During the same era, Jean de Nostre Dame (brother of the famous astrologer) published a French collection of troubadour biographies loosely based on the Provençal originals. A literary history of the troubadours—including their lives—was produced by the Abbé Millot some two hundred years later, an effort which apparently drew upon the earlier research of J. B. Lacurne de Sainte Palaye (see Gossman, *Medievalism*, pp. 163 ff.). By the nineteenth century, serious editions of the texts were being attempted by German and French philologists.

Nonetheless, the vidas remained little known within the tradition of European letters until the lifetime of Ezra Pound. Pound, an avid student and translator of Old Provençal, was obviously and willingly inspired by the troubadour's lives (see Wilhelm, *Later Cantos*, pp. 35–45). Echoes and even quotations of the vidas pervade his work, with the result that an increasing number of modern readers have become familiar with the texts. A few of the *Personae* treat troubadours, Pound combining details from the Provençal biographies with his own interpretations of their verses. In "Marvoil," the reader finds passages from Arnaut de Marueill's "life" (11) and in "Near Périgord" appears the tradition, found in the *vida*, of Bertran de Born's love of strife (17; see also *Personae*, pp. 22–24, 151–157; McDougal, pp. 45–51, 141–144).

Many of the *Cantos* show the similar, if indirect, influence of Old Provençal texts. Canto 4 recounts Peire Vidal's adventures disguised as a wolf (see the Razo in Boutière-Schutz, pp. 368–374) and recalls Guillem de Cabestaing's mistress jumping off a balcony as she avoids the blow of her jealous husband's sword (53). In Canto 5 Pound evokes the "lives" of three troubadours: Gausbert de Poicibot (39), Bernart de Ventadorn (14), and Peire de Maensac (73), while Cantos 6 and 29 chronicle the amorous affairs of Bernart de Ventadorn and Sordello, also told in Vidas 14 and 94.

Finally, and not surprisingly, Pound's interpretive essay, "Troubadours—Their Sorts and Conditions," also draws attention to the vidas. His exhortations in this text may inspire us all:

> If a man be so crotchety as to wish emotional, as well as intellectual, acquaintance with an age so out of fashion as the twelfth century, he may try in several ways to attain it. He may read the songs themselves from the old books— from the illuminated vellum—and he will learn what the troubadours meant to the folk of the century after their own. . . . Or [he] may walk the hill roads and river roads from Limoges and Charente to Dordogne and Narbonne . . . and learn . . . why such a man made war on such and such castles. Or he may learn the outlines of these events from the . . . 'lives of the troubadours' " (*Literary Essays*, pp. 95–96).

Editorial Policy for this Translation

Vida texts of varying accuracy—some of alarming unreliability—had been in print for over a century when the first critical edition appeared: Jean Boutière and A. H. Schutz, *Biographies des*

Troubadours (Paris: Nizet, 1950). There had been earlier editions by Raynouard, Mahn, and Chabaneau (see Select Bibliography). Although another critical edition exists (Favati, *Biografie Trovadoriche*), most scholars still prefer the French edition, which was revised in 1964. Following the majority opinion, I have also accepted the readings of Boutière and Schutz. In certain controversial passages, however, I have discussed Favati's text in the notes.

Few translations of the vidas are available to the modern reader. Boutière and Schutz provided French translations to their critical edition and a few other French and Spanish versions appear in anthologies (see Riquer, *Los Trovadores*). The only English translation of the vidas (Ida Farnell's in 1896) suffers not only from its archaic language but also from its inaccuracies.

In the translation presented here, the first modern English version, some literary elegance has been sacrificed for the sake of narrative and linguistic faithfulness. Following the vidas' peculiar syntactic constructions, I have maintained word order from the original texts as often as possible. In so doing, I have tried to preserve characteristic rhythms of the vida prose—at times halting and awkward, at times flowing and melodious. Nevertheless, on select occasions I have had to take liberties with the original text when the Old Provençal is unclear; this has meant filling out lines and in a few cases suppressing unnecessary or even confusing conjunctions. In the same spirit, certain Old Provençal terms for lyric compositions have been left untranslated (brief definitions are given in the glossary). Such decisions should enable those schooled in the language to consult the original texts, and at the same time permit readers unfamiliar with the biographies to grasp their particular character and mood.

The vidas in this volume have been arranged alphabetically, following the order established in the 1972 New York reprint of Boutière and Schutz' original 1950 anthology. A chronological list of troubadours appears in the Appendix.

Acknowledgments

This study and translation of the vidas is based on my Ph.D. dissertation (Yale University, 1976). Revision of the manuscript was funded by a grant from the American Council of Learned Societies (1978); I am grateful for their support. I also thank Yale University for the financial support it has lent me; awards from the A. Whitney Griswold Fund (1979, 1980) made rewriting this book possible, and a generous grant from the Frederick Hilles Fund (1981) allowed me to produce the manuscript with text-processing facilities of the Yale Computer Center.

The photographic reproductions of *chansonnier* illustrations are from the Bibliothèque Nationale, Paris. I acknowledge with thanks the right to reproduce them.

The success of the project owes much to Kenneth Hudson, who prepared the manuscript for publication and spent many hours editing at the terminal. We are both indebted to the staff of the Yale Computer Center, and to Marcia Weisz and Gary Moss in particular, for their unfailing help and willingness to experiment with our project.

Many colleagues and friends have read this book at different stages. Special thanks, however, are due to Lowry Nelson, Jr., Paul Zumthor, Thomas Bergin, William D. Paden, Nathaniel B. Smith, Leslie Topsfield, and Ulrich Mölk. Their comments and advice have been invaluable. I am grateful also to James J. Wilhelm for his careful editing of the manuscript.

For painstaking readings of the manuscript, editorial advice, and warm encouragement, I thank my husband, Brook Manville.

Select Bibliography

I. Major Texts and Critical Editions

Almqvist, Kurt. *Poésies du troubadour Guillem Adémar*. Uppsala: 1951.

Andraud, P. *La Vie et l'oeuvre de Raimon de Miraval*. Paris: 1902.

Appel, Carl. *Bernart von Ventadorn*. Halle: 1915.

──────. "L'enseignement de Garin lo Brun." *Revue des Langues Romanes*, 33 (1889), 404–32.

──────. *Die Lieder Bertrans von Born*. Halle: 1932.

──────. *Der Trobador Cadenet*. Halle: 1920.

──────. "Poésies provençales inédites tirées des manuscrits d'Italie." *Revue des Langues Romanes*, 34 (1890), 5–35; 39 (1896), 177–216; 40 (1897), 405–426.

Aston, S. C. *Peirol, Troubadour of Auvergne*. Cambridge, Eng.: 1953.

Audiau, Jean. *Nouvelle anthologie des troubadours*. Paris: 1928.

──────. *Les Poésies des quatre troubadours d'Ussel*. Paris: 1922.

Avalle, D'Arco S. *Peire Vidal: Poesie*. Milan-Naples: 1960.

Bertoni, Giulio. *I Trovatori d'Italia*. Modena: 1915.

Blasi, Ferruccio. *Le Poesie di Guillem de la Tor*. Geneva-Florence: 1934.

Bogin, Meg. *The Women Troubadours*. New York: 1976.

Bond, Gerald A. *The Poetry of William VII, Count of Poitiers, IX Duke of Aquitaine*. New York: 1982.

Boni, Marco. *Sordello: Le Poesie*. Bologna: 1954.

Boutière, Jean. "Peire Bremon Lo Tort." *Romania*, 54 (1928), 427–452.

──────. "Les poésies du troubadour Albertet." *Studi Medievali*, 10 (1937), 1–129.

————. "Le troubadour Guillem de Balaun." *Annales du Midi*, 48 (1936), 225–251.

————, and A. H. Schutz. *Biographies des Troubadours*. 1st ed. Toulouse: 1950; 2nd ed. Paris: 1964; rpt. New York: 1972 (based on 1950 ed.).

Braccini, M. *Rigaut de Barbezieux: Le canzoni, testo e commento*. Florence: 1960.

Brackney, E. M. "A Critical Edition of the Poems of Dalfin d'Alvernhe." Dissertation, University of Minnesota, 1937.

Branciforti, Francesco. *Il Canzonere di Lanfranco Cigala*. Florence: 1954.

Caboni, A. "Le Poesie di Uc de Mataplana." *Cultura Neolatina*, 1 (1941), 216–221.

Cavaliere, Alfredo. *Le Poesie di Peire Raimon de Tolosa*. Florence: 1935.

Chabaneau, Camille. *Les Biogaphies des Troubadours en Langue Provençale*. Toulouse: 1885.

Chambers, F. M. "Raimon de las Salas." *Essays in Honor of Louis Francis Solano*. Chapel Hill: 1970; 29–51.

Chaytor, H. J. *Les Chansons de Perdigon*. Paris: 1926.

————. *Savaric de Mauléon, Baron and Troubadour*. Cambridge, Eng.: 1939.

Coulet, Jules. *Le Troubadour Guillem de Montaignagol*. Toulouse: 1898.

De Lollis, C. "Bertran del Pojet, trovatore dell'età angioina." *Miscellanea in onore di Arturo Graf*. Bergamo: 1903; 706 ff.

Dejeanne, J.M.L. *Poésies complètes du troubadour Marcabru*. Toulouse: 1909.

Dumitrescu, Maria. *Poésies du troubadour Aimeric de Belenoi*. Paris: 1935.

Ernst, Willy. "Die Lieder des provenzalischen Trobadors Guiraut von Calanso". *Romanische Forschungen*, 44 (1930), 255–406.

Farnell, Ida. *The Lives of the Troubadours: Translated from the Mediaeval Provençal, with Introductory Matter and Notes, and with Specimens of their Poetry rendered into English*. London: 1896.

Favati, Guido. *Le Biografie trovadoriche: testi provenzali dei secoli XIII e XIV*. Bologna: 1961.

Finoli, A. M. "Le poesie di Guiraudo lo Ros." *Studi Medievali*, 15 (1974), 1–57.

Hill, R. T., T. G. Bergin, and others. *Anthology of the Provençal Trou-badours.* 2nd ed. rev. 2 vols. New Haven: 1973.

Huygens, R.B.C. *Accessus ad Auctores. Bernard d'Utrecht. Conrad d'Hir-sau: Dialogus Super Auctores.* Leiden: 1970.

Jaeschke, Hilde. *Der Trobador Elias Cairel.* Berlin: 1921.

Jeanroy, Alfred. *Jongleurs et troubadours gascons des XIIe et XIIIe siècles.* Paris: 1923.

————. *Les Poésies de Cercamon.* Paris: 1922.

————, and J. J. Salverda de Grave. *Poésies de Uc de Saint Circ.* Toulouse: 1913.

Johnston, Ronald C. *Les Poésies lyriques du troubadour Arnaut de Mar-ueil.* Paris: 1935.

Kjellman, Hilding. *Le Troubadour Raimon Jordan, Vicomte de Saint-An-tonin.* Uppsala-Paris: 1922.

Klein, Otto. *Der Troubadour Blacassetz.* Wiesbaden: 1887.

————. *Die Dichtungen des Mönchs von Montaudon.* Marburg: 1885.

Kolsen, Adolf. *Sämtliche Lieder des Troubadours Giraut de Bornelh.* 2 vols. Halle: 1910, 1935.

Kussler-Ratyé, Gabrielle. "Les chansons de la comtesse Béatrix de Dia." *Archivum Romanicum,* I (1917), 161–182.

Långfors, Arthur. *Les Chansons de Guillem de Cabestanh.* Paris: 1924.

Lavaud, René. *Les Poésies d'Arnaut Daniel.* Toulouse: 1910.

————. *Poésies complètes du troubadour Peire Cardenal (1180–1278).* Toulouse: 1957.

Lazar, Moshé. *Bernart de Ventadour, troubadour du XIIe siècle: chansons d'amour.* Paris: 1966.

Levy, Emil. *Der Troubadour Bertolome Zorzi.* Halle: 1883.

————. *Guilhem Figueira, ein provenzalischer Troubadour.* Berlin: 1880.

Linskill, Joseph. *The Poems of the Troubadour Raimbaut de Vaqueiras.* The Hague: 1964.

Mahn, C.A.F. *Biographieen der Troubadours in provenzalischer Sprache.* Berlin: 1878.

Monte, Alberto del. *Peire d'Alvernha: Liriche.* Turin: 1955.

Mouzat, J. D. *Les Poèmes de Gaucelm Faidit, troubadour du XIIe siècle.* Paris: 1965.

Müller, Johannes. "Die Gedichte des Guillem Augier Novella." *Zeitschrift für Romanische Philologie,* 23 (1899), 47–78; 27 (1903), 48 ff.

Napolski, Max von. *Leben und Werke des Trobadors Pons de Capduoill.* Halle: 1879.

Naudieth, Fritz. *Der Trobador Guilhem Magret.* Halle: 1914.

Newcombe, T. H. "The Troubadour Berenger de Palazol: A Critical Edition of his Poems." *Nottingham Medieval Studies,* 15 (1972), 54–95.

Nichols, Stephen G., et al. *The Songs of Bernart de Ventadorn.* Chapel Hill: 1962.

Nicholson, Derek T. *The Poems of the Troubadour Peire Rogier.* Manchester: 1976.

Paden, William D., Jr. "The Poems of the *Trobairitz* Na Castelloza." *Romance Philology,* 35 (1981), 159–182.

———, et al. *The Poems of the Troubadour Bertran de Born.* Berkeley: 1984.

Panvini, Bruno. *Giraldo di Bornelh, trovatore del sec. XII.* Catania: 1949.

Pattison, Walter T. *The Life and Works of the Troubadour Raimbaut d'Orange.* Minneapolis: 1952.

P.-C.: Pillet, Alfred, and Henry Carstens. *Bibliographie der Troubadours.* Halle: 1933; rpt. 1968.

Raupach, Manfred. "Elias Fonsalada Kritische Ausgabe." *Zeitschrift für Romanische Philologie,* 90 (1974), 141–173.

Raynouard, F.J.M. *Biographies des troubadours et appendice à leurs poésies imprimées dans les volumes précédents. Choix des poésies originales des Troubadours,* 5. Paris: 1820.

Ricketts, Peter. *Les Poésies de Guilhem de Montanhagol, troubadour provençal du XIIIe siècle.* Toronto: 1964.

Riquer, Martín de. *Guillem de Berguedà.* 2 vols. Abadía de Poblet: 1971.

———. *La Lírica de los trovadores.* Barcelona: 1948.

———. *Los Trovadores: Historia literaria y textos.* 3 vols. Barcelona: 1975.

Sakari, Aimo. *Poésies du troubadour Guillem de Saint-Didier.* Helsinki: 1956.

Salverda de Grave, J. J. *Le troubadour Bertran d'Alamanon.* Toulouse: 1902; rpt. New York: 1971.

Schultz-Gora, Oscar. *Die provenzalischen Dichterinnen, Biographieen und Texte.* Leipzig: 1888.

Schutz, A. H. *Poésies de Daude de Pradas.* Toulouse: 1933.

Shepard, W. P. *Les Poésies de Jausbert de Puycibot, troubadour du XIIIe siècle.* Paris: 1924.

————, and F. M. Chambers. *The Poems of Aimeric de Peguilhan.* Evanston: 1950.

Soltau, Otto. "Die Werke des Trobadors Blacatz." *Zeitschrift für Romanische Philologie,* 23 (1899), 201–248; 24 (1900), 33–60.

Stimming, Albert. *Bertran von Born.* 2nd ed. Halle: 1913.

Stronski, Stanislaw. *Le Troubadour Elias de Barjols.* Toulouse: 1906.

————. *Le Troubadour Folquet de Marseille.* Krakow: 1910.

Toja, Gianluigi. *Arnaut Daniel: Canzoni.* Florence: 1960.

Topsfield, L. T. *Les Poésies du troubadour Raimon de Miraval.* Paris: 1971.

Varvaro, Alberto. *Rigaut de Berbezilh: Liriche.* Bari: 1960.

Wilhelm, J. J. *The Poetry of Arnaut Daniel.* New York: 1981.

Wolf, George, and Roy Rosenstein. *The Poetry of Cercamon and Jaufre Rudel.* New York: 1983.

Zenker, Rudolf. *Die Gedichte des Folquet von Romans.* Halle: 1896.

II. Critical and Related Works

Alvar, Carlos. *La Poesía trovadoresca en España y Portugal.* Barcelona: 1977.

Anglade, Joseph. *Les Troubadours.* Paris: 1908.

Aston, S. C. "The Name of the Troubadour Dalfin d'Alvernhe." *French and Provençal Lexicography: Essays Presented to Honor A. H. Schutz.* Eds. U. T. Holmes and K. R. Scholberg. Columbus: 1964; 140–163.

Auerbach, Erich. *Literary Language and Its Public in Late Antiquity and in the Middle Ages.* New York: 1965.

Avalle, D'Arco S. *La Letteratura medievale in lingua d'oc nella sua tradizione manoscritta.* Torino: 1961.

Bec, P. *Là Langue occitane.* Paris: 1973.

Bertoni, Giulio. "Come fu che Peire Vidal divenne imperatore." *Giornale storico della letteratura italiana,* 65 (1915), 49–50.

Boutière, Jean. "Quelques observations sur le texte des *vidas* et des *razos* dans les chansonniers provençaux AB et IK." *French and Provençal Lexicography: Essays Presented to Honor A. H. Schutz.* Eds. U. T. Holmes and K. R. Scholberg. Columbus: 1964; 125–139.

———. "Les italianismes des 'Biographies' des troubadours." *Mélanges de littérature comparée et de philologie offerts à M. Brahmer.* Warsaw: 1967; 93–107.

———. "Les 3e personnes du singulier en -a des 'Biographies' des Troubadours." *Actes et Mémoires du IIIe Congrès International de Langue et Littérature d'Oc.* Bordeaux: 1961; 1–11.

Brunel, Clovis. *Bibliographie des manuscrits littéraires en ancien provençal.* Paris: 1935.

———. "Les Troubadours Azemar Jordan et Uc Brunenc." *Romania,* 52 (1926), 505–508.

Camproux, Charles. *Histoire de la littérature occitane.* Paris: 1953.

Chaytor, H. J. *From Script to Print.* 1945; rpt. 1977.

Cravayat, Paul. "Les origines du troubadour J. Rudel." *Romania,* 74 (1950), 166–179.

Dardano, Maurizio. *Lingua e tecnica narrativa nel Duecento.* Rome: 1969.

Delahaye, Hippolyte. *Les Légendes hagiographiques.* Brussels: 1955.

Egan, Margarita. "The Old Provençal *Vidas*: A Textural Analysis." Dissertation, Yale, 1976.

———. " 'Razo' and 'Novella': A Case Study in Narrative Forms." *Medioevo Romanzo,* 6 (1979), 302–314.

———. "Commentary, *Vitae poetae* and *Vida*: Latin and Old Provençal 'Lives of Poets.' " *Romance Philology,* 37 (1983–84), 36–48.

Elcock, W. D. *The Romance Languages.* 2nd ed. London: 1975.

Faral, Edmond. "La Pastourelle." *Romania,* 49 (1923), 204–259.

Fernandez Pereiro, N.G.B. de. *Originalidad y sinceridad en la poesía de amor trovadoresca.* La Plata: 1968.

Frank, István. "Tomier e Palazi, troubadours tarasconnais." *Romania, 78* (1957), 46–85.

Ghellinck, J. de. *Littérature latine au Moyen Age.* Hildesheim: 1969.

Goldin, Frederick. *The Mirror of Narcissus in the Courtly Love Lyric.* Ithaca, N.Y.: 1967.

Gossman, Lionel. *Medievalism and the Ideologies of the Enlightenment.* Baltimore: 1968.

Guida, Saverno. "Per la biografia di Gui de Cavaillon e di Bertran Folco d'Avignon." *Cultura Neolatina, 32* (1972), 189–210.

Hauvette, Henri. "La 39ème nouvelle du Décaméron et la légende du Coeur Mangé." *Romania, 16* (1912), 184–205.

Hoepffner, Ernest. "La Biographie de Perdigon." *Romania, 53* (1927), 343–364.

Hunt, R. W. "The Introductions to the 'Artes' in the Twelfth Century." *Studia Mediaevalia in honorem admodum reverendi patris Raymundi Josephi Martin.* Bruges: 1948; 85–112.

Jeanroy, Alfred. *La Poésie lyrique des troubadours.* 2 vols. Toulouse: 1934.

Köhler, Erich. "Marcabrus *L'autrier jost'una sebissa* und das Problem der Pastourelle." *Romanistisches Jahrbuch, 5* (1952), 256–268.

Lafont, Robert. *Nouvelle histoire de la littérature occitane.* Paris: 1970.

Lejeune, Rita. "Ce qu'il faut croire des 'Biographies' provençales: La Louve de Pennautier." *Le Moyen Age, 69* (1939), 233–249.

———. "Le chien Pan-perdu et le chat Marcabru de Frédéric Mistral." *Mélanges de Philologie Romane dédiés à la mémoire de Jean Boutière.* 2 vols. Liège: 1971; II, 801–806.

Lewis, C. S. *Allegory of Love.* London: 1936.

Macedonia, John. "Motif-Index of the Biographies of the Troubadours." Dissertation, Ohio State, 1961.

Makin, Peter. *Provence and Pound.* Berkeley: 1978.

Marrou, H. I. *Les Troubadours.* Paris: 1971.

Marshall, J. H. *The 'Razos de Trobar' of Raimon Vidal.* London: 1972.

McDougal, S. Y. *Ezra Pound and the Troubadour Tradition.* Princeton: 1972.

Méjean, Suzanne. "Contribution à l'étude du 'sirventes joglaresc.' "

Mélanges de Philologie Romane dédiés à la mémoire de Jean Boutière. 2 vols. Liège: 1971; I, 377–395.

Monteverdi, Angelo. "Che cos'è il 'Novellino'?" *Studi e saggi sulla letteratura italiana dei primi secoli.* Milan-Naples: 1954.

Neuschäfer, H. J. "Die Herzmäre in der altprovenzalischen *vida* und in der Novelle Boccaccios." *Poetica,* 2 (1968), 38–47.

Novati, Francesco. "Un'avventura di Peire Vidal." *Romania,* 21 (1892), 78–81.

Niestroy, Erich. *Der Trobador Pistoleta.* Halle: 1914.

Ong, Walter J. *Orality and Literacy: the Technologizing of the Word.* London: 1982.

Paden, William D., Jr. "L'emploi vicaire du présent verbal dans les plus anciens textes narratifs romans." *Atti. XIV Congresso Internazionale di Linguistica e Filologia Romanza* (1967), 545–557.

Panvini, Bruno. *Le Biografie provenzali: valore e attendibilità.* Florence: 1952.

Paris, Gaston. "Jaufre Rudel." *Revue Historique,* 53 (1893), 225–260.

P.-C.: See Pillet in Section I.

Pizzorusso, V. Bertolucci. "Il grado zero della retorica nella vida di Jaufre Rudel." *Studi Mediolatini e Volgari, 18* (1970), 7–26.

Pound, Ezra. *Cantos.* New York: 1972.

———. *Literary Essays,* ed. T. S. Eliot. London: 1954; rpt. New York: 1972.

———. *Personae.* New York: 1971.

Quain, E. A. "The Medieval *accessus ad auctores.*" *Traditio, 3* (1945), 215–264.

Roncaglia, Aurelio. *La Lingua dei Trovatori.* Rome: 1965.

Sakari, Aimo. "Azalais de Porcairagues." *Neuphilologische Mitteilungen,* 50 (1949), 23–43, 56–87, 174–198.

Schutz, A. H. "A Preliminary Study of *trobar e entendre,* an Expression in Mediaeval Aesthetics." *Romanic Review,* 23 (1932), 129–132.

———. "Were the *vidas* and *razos* Recited?" *Studies in Philology, 36* (1939), 565–570.

———. "Where Were the Provençal *vidas* and *razos* Written?" *Modern Philology*, *35* (1938), 225–232.

Strayer, J. *The Albigensian Crusade*. New York: 1971.

Stronski, Stanislaw. "Recherches historiques sur quelques protecteurs des troubadours." *Annales du Midi*, *18* (1906), 473 ff.; *19* (1907), 40 ff.

———. *La Poésie et la réalité aux temps des troubadours*. Oxford: 1943.

———. *Le Troubadour Folquet de Marseille*. Krakow: 1910.

Sumption, John. *The Albigensian Crusade*. London: 1978.

Topsfield, L. T. *Troubadours and Love*. Cambridge, Eng.: 1973.

Wakefield, W. L. *Heresy, Crusade, and Inquisition in Southern France, 1100–1250*. Berkeley: 1974.

Wilhelm, J. J. *The Cruelest Month: Spring, Nature and Love in Classical and Medieval Lyrics*. New Haven: 1965.

———. *Seven Troubadours: The Creators of Modern Verse*. University Park, Pa.: 1970.

———. *The Later Cantos of Ezra Pound*. New York: 1977.

Zanders, Josef. *Die Altprovenzalische Prosanovelle. Eine litterar-historische Kritik der Trobador-Biographieen*. Halle: 1913.

Zumthor, Paul. *Essai de poétique médiévale*. Paris: 1972.

The Vidas
of the
Troubadours

1. ADEMAR LO NEGRE

Lord Aimar lo Negre[1] was from Château-Vieux of Albi.[2]
He was a courtly man and eloquent. And he was well honored
among high society, by King Pedro of Aragon[3] and by Count
Raimon de Toulouse, the one who was dispossessed,[4] who gave
him houses and land in Toulouse. And he composed songs as
well as he knew how. And here are written some of his
songs.

[1] Ademar le Noir (the Black).
[2] Château-Vieux, canton of Pouyastruc, arrondissement of
Tarbes (Tarn), was under the suzerainty of the
viscounts of Albi during the 12th century.
[3] Pedro II (1196-1213), son and successor to Alfonso II,
was the patron of many troubadours.
[4] Raimon VI (1194-1222) was dispossessed of his estate
by the Lateran Council after the Albigensian Crusade
(1215).

2. AIMERIC DE BELENOI

Lord Aimeric de Belenoi[1] was from Bordelais[2] from a
castle named Lesparre,[3] the nephew of Master Peire de
Corbiac.[4] He was a cleric and became a minstrel and
invented good songs, which were beautiful and charming,
about a lady from Gascony named Gentil de Rieux.[5] And for
her he stayed in that region for a long time; later he went
to Catalonia and was there until he died. And here are
written some of his songs.

[1] Unknown place. See the poet's verses in Maria
Dumitrescu, *Poésies du troubadour Aimeric de Belenoi*
(Paris, 1935).
[2] Old *Metropolis civitas Burdigalensium*, today
comprising most of the department of Gironde and the

northern region of the department of Landes.

[3] Today seat of a canton in the arrondissement of Bordeaux (Gironde).

[4] Troubadour (Pillet-Carstens, *Bibliographie* [hereafter P.-C.] 338) who composed a didactic poem (*Thezaur*) and a song to the Virgin.

[5] Gentilis de Genciaco (Gensac-Saint-Julien, in the canton of Rieux) wife of Raimon de Benque. Rieux is the seat of a canton in the arrondissement of Toulouse (Haute-Garonne).

3. AIMERIC DE PEGUILHAN

Lord Aimeric de Peguilhan[1] was from Toulouse, the son of a burgher who was a merchant and had cloth to sell. He learned songs and *sirventes*, but he sang very badly. And he fell in love with a burgher, his neighbor. And this love taught him how to invent poetry. And he composed many good songs about her. And the husband of the lady quarreled with him and dishonored him. And Lord Aimeric took revenge and struck him on the head with a sword. For this reason it was necessary for him to leave Toulouse and go into exile.

And he went to Catalonia. And Lord Guillem de Berguedan[2] welcomed him, and he exalted him in his invention of poetry, in the first song he composed. And Guillem made him a minstrel and gave him his palfrey and his clothing. And he introduced him to King Anfos de Castilla[3] who increased his equipment and his honor. And he was in those regions for a long time.

Later he went to Lombardy, where all the notable men granted him great honor. And he ended his days in Lombardy.

[1] In the arrondissement of Saint-Gaudens (Haute-Garonne). This poet's works appear in W. P. Shepard and F. M. Chambers, *The Poems of Aimeric de Peguillan* (Evanston, 1950).

[2] The troubadour Guillem de Berguedan (see Vida 52) exchanged a *partimen* with Aimeric.
[3] Alfonso VIII of Castile (1158-1214).

B. AIMERIC DE PEGUILHAN
(Continuation from manuscript *R*)

And it so happened that the husband of the lady recovered from his wound and he went to San Jacme.[1] Lord Aimeric learned this and desired to go into Toulouse. And he came to the king and told him that, if it pleased him, he would like to see the Marquis of Montferrat.[2] And the king gave him permission to go, and furnished him well with equipment of all kinds. Lord Aimeric told the king that he wished to pass through Toulouse, but he was concerned about what the king knew; for the king was aware of all the facts and could see that the lady's love attracted Aimeric. And the king gave him an escort up to Montpellier. And he Aimeric made known to his companions all the facts, and asked them to help him, for he wished to see his lady while pretending to be sick. And they assured him that they would do everything that he commanded.

And when they were in Toulouse, the companions asked where the burgher's house was, and it was shown to them. And they found the lady and told her that a relative of the King of Castile was sick, that he was going on a pilgrimage, and that he would like to be allowed into her house. She answered that he would be served and honored there. Lord Aimeric came at night, and his companions lay him on a beautiful bed. And the following day Lord Aimeric sent for the lady. And the lady came to the room and recognized Lord Aimeric, and was very astonished, and asked him how he had managed to enter Toulouse. And he told her that [he had done it] because of his love. And he told her everything. And the lady pretended to cover him with the cloth and kissed him. From here on, I do not know what happened, except that Lord Aimeric stayed there for ten days under the pretext of his illness. And when he left there, he went to the marquis, where he was well greeted. And here you will find some of his works.

3

[1] Santiago de Compostela in Galicia, Spain, where the relics of Saint James were venerated after the reign of Alfonso the chaste of Castile (791-835).

[2] Guillaume IV of Montferrat (1207-1223), mentioned in a crusade song (P.-C. 10.11) and a love song (P.-C. 10.43) dating from 1213 and 1225 respectively.

4. AIMERIC DE SARLAT

Lord Aimeric de Sarlat was from Perigord, from a rich town called Sarlat.[1] And he became a minstrel, and he was very clever at reciting and at creating, and he became an inventor of poetry. But he composed only one song.

[1] Sarlat is the seat of an arrondissement in Dordogne.

5. ALBERTET CAILLA

Albertet Cailla was a minstrel from the Albigeois.[1] He was a man of slight worth, but he was loved by his neighbors and by the ladies of the Albigeois. And he composed a good song and he composed *sirventes*. But he never left his own region.

[1] (Albeges or Albezet), the region of Albi (*Albiga*), today the department of Tarn.

6. ALBERTET DE SESTARO

Albertet was from Gapençais,[1] son of a minstrel called Lord Asar[2] who was an inventor of poetry and composed good little songs. And Albertet also composed plenty of songs which had good melodies and words of slight worth. He was well esteemed near and far because of the good melodies he composed, and he was a very good minstrel in the court and a pleasing conversationalist among the people. And he spent a long time in Orange and became rich. And later he went to Sisteron[3] to stay, and there he ended his days.

[1] Region around Gap (Hautes-Alpes).
[2] Unknown jongleur, one of whose songs perhaps survives (P.-C. 44.1). See J. Boutière, *Les Poésies du Troubadour Albertet* (Torino, 1937), 1-129; in particular, p. 10.
[3] Sisteron is the seat of a canton in the arrondissement of Forcalquier (Basses-Alpes) near the Gapençais.

7. ALBERT MARQUES

Marquis Albert[1] was from [the family of] the Marquis of Malaspina. He was a valiant man, generous, courtly, and learned. And he knew well how to compose couplets and *sirventes* and songs.

[1] Marquis Albert Malaspina (b. 1160-1165) was the son of Obizzo I, the Great. Like his brother-in-law Boniface of Montferrat and his nephews Conrad I and Guillaume Malaspina, Albert was an enthusiastic patron of troubadours.

8. ALMUC DE CASTELNOU and ISEUT DE CAPIEU

(Razo of P.-C. 20.2 and 253.1.)

Lady Iseut de Chapieu[1] begged my lady Almodis de Châteauneuf[2] that she pardon Lord Gigo de Tournon,[3] who was her knight, and who had committed a great fault against her. And he did not repent of it or ask to be forgiven:

Lady Almodis, if it would please you,
I would like to ask you this:
That instead of anger and unwillingness
You have mercy on him
Who sighs and laments
And dies languishing and complains
And humbly seeks forgiveness,
For I make an oath for him:
That he will refrain from wrongdoing
If you will end all strife with him.[4]

And my lady Almodis, who loved Lord Gigo de Tornon, was also very sorrowful because he did not ask forgiveness. And she answered my lady Lady Iseut in the way this couplet says:

Lady Iseut, if I knew
That he repented of the great deceit
He did to me,
It would well be right for me
To be merciful. But it would not be right,
Since he is not sorry about the wrong,
Nor does he repent of it
To ever have any pity.
Still, if you make him repent
You can easily change my mind.[5]

---

[1] Chapieu (*Castrum de Capione*) is in the commune of Lanvejouls, arrondissement of Mende (Lozère).

[2] Almodis (also Almois) was married to Guigne de Châteauneuf-de-Raudon in the arrondissement of Mende (Lozère).

[3] Probably Gui de Tournon, lord of Tournon in Vivarais.

6

See Boutière-Schutz, p. 424.
[4] Dompna N'Almue[i]s, si.ous plages,
Be.us volgra prejar d'aitan:
Qe l'ira e.l mal talan
Vos fezes fenir merces
De lui, qe sospir'e plaing
E muor languen e.s complaing
Qe.us fatz per lui sagramen,
Si tot li voletz fenir,
Q'el si gart meils de faillir. (P.-C. 253.1)
See editions of Almuc de Castelnou's poem: O.
Schultz-Gora, p. 25, and Bogin, pp. 92-93.
[5] Dompna N'Iseuz, s'ieu saubes
Q'el se pentis de l'engan
Q'el a fait vas mi tan gran,
Ben fora dreichz q'eu n'agues
Merces; mas a mi no.s taing,
Pos qe del tort no s'afraing
Ni.s pentis del faillimen,
Qe n'aia mais chausimen;
Mas si vos faitz lui pentir,
Leu podes mi convertir. (P.-C. 20.2)
See Schultz-Gora, p. 12, and Bogin, pp. 92-93.

9. AMFOS (ALFONSO) OF ARAGON

The King of Aragon,[1] the one who invented poetry, was
called Amfos. And he was the first king there was in
Aragon; he was the son of Lord Raimon Berengar,[2] who was
the Count of Barcelona, and who conquered the kingdom of
Aragon and took it from the Saracens.[3] And he went to Rome
to be crowned. He died in Piemonte[4] in the town of
Saint-Dalmac.[5] And his son Amfos was made king. He was the
father of King Pedro,[6] who was the father of King Jaime.[7]

[1] Alfonso I, born in 1152 or 1158, became Count of
Barcelona in 1162, King of Aragon (as Alfonso II) in
1164, and Count of Provence in 1166. He died in 1196.

7

[2] Raimon-Berengar IV.
[3] Alfonso did not conquer the Saracens, but he did fight against them in 1148.
[4] The Piedmont region of Italy.
[5] Saint-Dalmac is today Borgo San Dalmazzo, south of Coni. Raimon died there in 1162.
[6] Pedro II of Aragon (1196-1213). See Vida 1, note 3.
[7] Jaime I (1213-1276) called "The Conqueror."

10. ARNAUT DANIEL

Arnaut Daniel came from the same region as Lord Arnaut de Meruoill,[1] from the bishopric of Perigord, from a castle named Ribérac,[2] and he was a noble man. And he learned letters well and he took delight in inventing poetry. And he abandoned letters and became a minstrel; and he developed a way of inventing with difficult rhymes, which is why his songs are not easy to understand or to learn. And he loved a high-born lady from Gascony, wife of Lord Guillem de Bouvilla.[3] But it was not believed that the lady gave him pleasure in love, which is why he says:

I am Arnaut who gathers the wind
and hunts the hare with an ox
and swims against the tide.[4]

[1] See Vida 11. Other biographical facts concerning Arnaut are discussed in R. Lavaud, *Les Poésies d'Arnaut Daniel* (Toulouse, 1910), pp. 117-121, and more recently in the editions of J. J. Wilhelm, *The Poetry of Arnaut Daniel* (New York, 1981) and G. Toja, *Arnaut Daniel: Canzoni* (Florence, 1960). See also for references to this troubadour, Dante's *Purgatorio* 27, T. S. Eliot's dedication of "Wasteland" to Pound, and Pound's *Cantos*.
[2] Seat of a canton in the arrondissement of Périgueux (Dordogne).

[3] Guillem de Bouville? He and his wife are unknown.
See Boutière-Schutz, p. 61, note 5.

[4] Eu son Arnautz qu'amas l'aura
E chatz la lebre ab lo bou
E nadi contra suberna. (P.-C. 29.10)

11. ARNAUT DE MARUEIL (MERUOILL)

Arnaut de Marueil was from the bishopric of Perigord,[1] from a castle called Marueil,[2] and he was a cleric of humble origin. And because he could not live by his letters, he traveled around the world. And he invented poetry and created well. And destiny and fortune led him to the court of the Countess of Burlatz,[3] who was the daughter of the valiant Count Raimon and wife of the Viscount of Béziers,[4] who was called Taillefer.

This Lord Arnaut was a handsome man, and he sang well and he read Provençal.[5] And the countess did much for him and granted him great honor. And he fell in love with her and also composed songs about the countess. But he did not dare tell her or anyone else that he himself had composed them; rather he would say that someone else had done so.

But it so happened that Love compelled him to compose a song which begins:

The noble deportment.[6]

In this song he revealed to her the love he had for her. And the countess did not avoid him, but rather listened to his requests and welcomed them, and was grateful for them. And she furnished him raiment and conferred upon him great honor and encouraged him to invent poetry about her. And he became her honorable courtier. And so he composed many good songs about the countess which show that he received great good and great ill from her.

[1] Today the departments of Dordogne and Lot-et-Garonne.

[2] Marueil-sur-Belle, in the arrondissement of Nontron (Dordogne).

[3] Azalais of Toulouse, daughter of Count Raimon V, was brought up in a castle of Burlatz, canton of Roquecourbe, (Tarn). She married the viscount of Béziers and Carcassonne, Roger II--called Taillefer--in 1171.

[4] Seat of an arrondissement in Hérault.

[5] *Lisia romans* has been translated by Boutière-Schutz as "lisait bien les oeuvres littéraires" (p. 34), but could also mean that he read anything written in the vernacular.

[6] La franca captenensa. (P.-C. 30.15)
For other poems by Arnaut, see Ronald C. Johnston, *Les Poésies lyriques du troubadour Arnaut de Marueil* (Paris, 1935). See also F. Goldin, *The Mirror of Narcissus* (Ithaca, 1967), pp. 82-92 for discussion of Arnaut's love poetry.

12. AZALAIS DE PORCAIRAGUES

Lady Azalais de Porcairagues[1] was from the region of Montpellier, a noble and learned lady. And she fell in love with Lord Gui Guerrejat,[2] who was the brother of Lord Guillem de Montpellier. And the lady knew how to invent poems, and she composed many good songs about him.

[1] Either Pourcairagues, in the commune of La Salle-de-Gardon, arrondissement of Alès, canton of La Grand-Combe (Gard), or Portiragues, in the canton of Béziers (Hérault). For further details, see A. Sakari, "Azalais de Porcairagues," *Neuphilologisches Mitteilungen*, 50 (1949), 23-43, 56-87, 174-198, and Schultz-Gora, p. 16.

[2] Son of Guillaume VI, nicknamed Guerrejat (meaning "warrior"), who died in 1177. His brother was Guillaume VII, lord of Montpellier.

13. BERENGUIER DE PALAZOL

Berenguier de Palazol[1] was from Catalonia, from the county of Roussillon.[2] He was a poor knight, but able and learned and skilled at arms. And he invented good songs, and he sang about Lady Ermessen d'Avinyo,[3] wife of Lord Arnaut d'Avinyo, who was the son of Lady Maria de Peiralada.[4]

[1] Paillol is today in the arrondissement of Céret (Pyrénées-Orientales). Palazol (or Parason, Palou, etc.) is a Provençal adaptation of the catalan *Palol*, according to M. Riquer, *Los Trovadores* I, 300-01. See also T. H. Newcombe, "The Troubadour Berenger de Palazol: A Critical Edition of his Poems," *Nottingham Medieval Studies*, 15 (1971), 54-95.

[2] Ancient county in the south of Languedoc.

[3] Unknown lady. Avinyo is a village in Besalù in Catalonia.

[4] This lady is probably confused with Maria domina de Petralata, mother of Soremonda, Raimon de Castel-Roussillon's wife, and lover of Guillem de Cabestaing (Vida 53).

14. BERNART DE VENTADORN

A. Version of manuscripts *ABEIKRSg*

Bernart de Ventadorn[1] was from Limousin,[2] from the castle of Ventadour.[3] He was a man of humble origin, the son of a servant who was a baker, and who heated the oven to bake the bread of the castle. And he became a handsome and an able man, and he knew how to sing and how to invent poetry well, and he became courtly and learned.

And the Viscount of Ventadour,[4] his lord, grew very fond of him and of his inventing and his singing, and greatly honored him. And the Viscount of Ventadour had a wife who was young, noble, and lively. And she also grew fond of Bernart and of his songs, and fell in love with him. And he fell in love with the lady, and composed his songs and his poems about her, about the love which he had for her, and about her merit. Their love lasted a long time before the viscount or other people became aware of it. And when the viscount perceived it, he banished Bernart from him and had his wife locked up and guarded. And the lady then gave Lord Bernart permission so that he would go away and leave that region.

And he left and went to the Duchess of Normandy,[5] who was young and of merit, and who understood merit and honor and beautiful words of praise. And, the songs and the poems of Lord Bernart pleased her very much, and she received him and welcomed him very well. He was in her court for a long time, and he fell in love with her, and she with him. And he composed many good songs about her. And while he was with her, King Henry of England[6] took her for his wife and also moved her away from Normandy and took her to England.

Lord Bernart remained here, sad and grieving, and he came to the good Count Raimon of Toulouse[7] and stayed with him until the count died. And Lord Bernart, on account of the sadness he felt, joined the order of Dalon,[8] and there he died.

And what I, Lord Uc de Saint Circ,[9] have written about him was told to me by the viscount Lord Ebles de Ventadorn,[10] who was the son of the viscountess whom Lord Bernart loved. And Bernart composed these songs which you will hear and which are written below.

---

[1] Major editions of Bernart de Ventadorn's verse: S. G. Nichols et al., *The Songs of Bernart de Ventadorn* (Chapel Hill, 1962); M. Lazar, *Bernart de Ventadour, troubadour du XIIe siècle: chansons d'amour* (Paris, 1966); C. Appel, *Bernart von Ventadorn* (Halle, 1915). See Ezra Pound's Cantos 6, 20, and 92 for references to Bernart; J. J. Wilhelm, *The Cruelest Month* (New Haven-London, 1965), pp. 151-193 for discussion of Bernart's poetics.
[2] Region and viscounty around Limoges, today the departments of Corrèze and Haute-Vienne.

[3] Ventadour is in the arrondissement of Tulle (Corrèze).
[4] Ebles III of Ventadour (1148-70) was first married to Marguerite of Turenne and later to Alais of Montpellier.
[5] Eleanor of Aquitaine did not become Duchess of Normandy, however, until after her marriage to Henry Plantagenet in 1152.
[6] Henry II Plantagenet (1154-1189).
[7] Raimon V of Toulouse (1148-1194).
[8] Dalon, in the canton of Hautefort (Dordogne). Site of a Cistercian abbey where Bertran de Born also ended his life.
[9] Although he is not mentioned in all the manuscripts, Uc is probably the author of this vida. See Boutière-Schutz, p. 25, note 8, and Vida 101.
[10] Ebles IV of Ventadour, son of Ebles III.

B. Version of manuscript N^2

Bernart de Ventadorn was from Limousin, from the castle of Ventadour. He was of humble origin, the son of a servant and of a woman baker, as Peire d'Alvernhe says of him in his song, where he speaks ill of all the troubadors:

As for the third, Bernart de Ventadorn,
Who is less than a palm shorter than Borneill,
His father was a good servant
Handy with a laburnum bow.
And his mother tended the oven
And the father brought the firewood.[1]

But, whoever's son he was, God gave him a handsome and pleasing appearance and a noble heart from which naturally emanated nobility, and He gave him wit and knowledge and courtesy and noble conversation. And he possessed subtlety and the skill of inventing good words and joyous melodies.

And he fell in love with the Viscountess of Ventadour, wife of his lord. And God granted him such good fortune because of his good conduct and his joyous invention, that she loved him beyond measure, such that she did not pay attention to reason, or nobility, or honor, or merit, or blame, but she abandoned reason and followed her desire, as Lord Arnaut de Meruoill says:

I consider joy and forget folly
I flee my reason and follow my desire[2]

and as Gui d'Uisel says also:

For thus it happens to a fine lover
That reason is impotent against desire.[3]

And he was honored and esteemed by all high society, and his songs were honored and welcome. And he was seen and heard and received very gladly, and he was granted great honor and great presents by the great barons and by the great men, among whom he traveled about in great costume and in great honor.

Their love lasted for a very long time before the viscount, her husband, perceived it. And when he perceived it, he was very sorrowful and sad, and he made the viscountess, his wife, very sad and very sorrowful. And he ordered her to take leave of Bernart de Ventadorn, that he should leave his territory.

And he left and went to Normandy, to the duchess who was then mistress of the Normans and who was young and lively, and of great merit and fame, and of great power, and who understood much about honor and merit. And she received him with great pleasure and with great honor, and was very happy at his arrival, and made him lord and master of all her court. And just as he had fallen in love with the wife of his lord, he fell in love with the duchess, and she with him.

For a long time he received great joy from her and great happiness, until she took the King Henry of England for her husband, who took her across the arm of the sea of England[4] so that he never saw her again, or received her messages. So afterwards because of the grief and the sadness he felt about her, he became a monk in the abbey of Dalon, and here he endured until the end.

14

[1] Lo terz Bernartz de Ventadorn,
Q'es meindre d'un Borneil un dorn;
En son paire ac bon sirven
Qe portav'ades arc d'alborn
E sa vair'escaudava.1 forn,
E.1 pair'dusia 1'essermen. (P.-C. 323.11)
See also Vida 67.
[2] Consir lo joi et oblit la foudat
E fuc mon sen e sec ma voluntat (P.-C. 30.23)
See also Vida 11.
[3] Q'enaissi s'aven de fin aman,
Qe.1 sens non a poder contra.1 talan. (P.-C. 194.3)
See also Vida 45.
[4] La Manche, the English Channel.

15. BERTOLOME ZORZI

A. Version of manuscript *A*

Bertolome Zorzi[1] was a noble man, a merchant from
Venice. And he was a good inventor of poems. And it so
happened that, as he was going from Venice to Romania[2] with
many other merchants who were from that city I mentioned to
you, he and all the other merchants who were with him in the
ship were apprehended one night by the Genoese. For at that
time there was a great war between the Venetians and the
Genoese. And all the men from the ship I told you about
were taken prisoners to Genoa. And while he was in prison,
he composed many good songs, and he also composed many
tensos with Lord Bonifaci Calvo[3] from Genoa.

And it so happened that peace was declared among the
Venetians and the Genoese, and Lord Bertolome Zorzi and all
the others left prison. And when these prisoners returned
to Venice, Lord Bertolome Zorzi was made castellan of Coron
and of Modon[4] in a rich place in Romania which belongs to
the Venetians--by my lord the Duke of Venice. And there he
fell in love with a noble lady of that region. And there he
ended his days and died.

15

[1] For an edition of his works, see E. Levy, *Der Troubadour Bertolome Zorzi* (Halle, 1883).

[2] The Byzantine Empire.

[3] All we know of this troubadour's life is from Zorzi's vida, although with Lanfranc Cigala he is the most notable Genoese troubadour.

[4] Koroni and Methoni, Greek ports on the southwestern peninsula of Morea.

B. Version of manuscripts *IKd*

Lord Bertolome Zorzi was a noble man from the city of Venice. He was a learned man of natural wit. And he knew how to invent poetry and how to sing well. And it so happened that one time he went around the world. And the Genoese, who were waging a war against the Venetians, seized him and took him prisoner to their land. And while he was in prison, Lord Bonifaci Calvo composed this *sirventes*, which is written below and begins:

It matters little to me if I am not esteemed[1]

blaming the Genoese for letting the Venetians vanquish them, and saying shameful things about them. Therefore, Lord Bertolome Zorzi composed another *sirventes*, which is written here below, and which begins:

I was very much surprised by a song[2]

justifying the Venetians and blaming the Genoese. Therefore Lord Bonifaci Calvo considered himself at fault for what he had said about this. So they turned to one another and became great friends. Lord Bertolome Zorzi stayed in prison for a long time, about seven years. And when he left prison, he went to Venice. And his community sent him as a castellan to a castle called Coron. And there he ended his days.

[1] Ges no m'es greu, s'ieu non sui ren prezatz (P.-C. 101.7).

16

² Molt me sui fort d'un chant mer[a]veillatz (P.-C. 74.10)

16. BERTRAN D'ALAMANON

Bertran d'Alamanon[1] was from Provence, the son of Lord Pons de Brugières.[2] He was a courtly knight and an eloquent speaker. And he composed good *tensos* and *sirventes*.

[1] Lamanon is a canton of Eyguières (Bouches-du-Rhône). For an edition of the poet's verses, see J. J. Salverda de Grave, *Le Troubadour Bertran D'Alamanon* (Toulouse, 1902).
[2] Unknown person. Brugières could be 1) a town in the arrondissement of Toulouse (Haute-Garonne); 2) La Bruguière, in the arrondissement of Uzès (Gard); or 3) Bruguière-Bezacoul, in the arrondissement of Castres (Tarn).

17. BERTRAN DE BORN

A. Version of manuscipts *ABFIK*

Bertran de Born[1] was a castellan from the bishopric of Perigord, and he was the lord of a castle called Hautefort. He was at war with his neighbors all the time, with the count of Perigord,[2] and with the viscount of Limoges,[3] and with his brother Constantine, and with Richard[4] as long as he was Count of Poitiers. He was a good knight and a good warrior, and a good lover of ladies, and a good inventor of

poetry, and he was wise and eloquent, and he knew well how
to deal with good and with evil men. He influenced,
whenever he wished, King Henry[5] and his son; but he always
wanted them to be at war with one another, the father, the
son, and the brother, one against the other. And he always
wanted the King of France[6] and the King of England to be at
war with each other. And if they had peace or a truce, he
would at once make an effort with his *sirventes* to undo the
peace, and to show how each one of them was being dishonored
by that peace. Thus he reaped much gain and much loss.

[1] Born refers to the land in the commune of Salagnac,
canton of Hautefort, arrondissement of Périgueux
(Dordogne). Major edition of Bertran de Born's 39
poems: C. Appel, *Die Lieder Bertrans von Born* (Halle,
1932); A. Stimming, *Bertran von Born*, 2nd ed. (Halle,
1918); W. D. Paden, Jr., et al., *The Poems of the
Troubadour Bertran de Born* (Berkeley, 1983). This
poet is depicted in Dante's *Inferno* 28, and in Pound's
monologues "Near Perigord" and "Sestina: Altaforte" in
Personae. For discussion of Bertran's role in the
work of Pound, see P. Makin, *Provence and Pound*
(Berkeley, 1978), p. 42 ff.

[2] Elias VI Talairan, count of Perigord from 1158-66 (?)
to 1203, is mentioned in two of Bertran's poems (see
A. Stimming, *Bertran von Born*, nos. 2 [v. 36] and 3
[v. 12]).

[3] Aimar V, Viscount of Limoges (1138-1199), is mentioned
in a few poems (see Stimming, Nos. 10, 14, 27).

[4] Richard the Lion-Hearted was Count of Poitiers from
1169 to 1189, when he succeeded his father Henry II to
the throne of England.

[5] Henry II Plantagenet (1154-1189).

[6] Philippe-Auguste (1180-1222).

B. Version of manuscripts *ER*

   Bertran de Born was from Limousin,[1] viscount of
Hautefort,[2] where he had close to a thousand men. And he
had brothers and was planning to rob them of their
inheritance, if it had not been for the King of England.[3]

He was a very good inventor of *sirventes*, and he never
composed more than two songs; and the King of Aragon[4]
proposed a marriage of the songs of Lord Guiraut de Borneill
to Bertran's *sirventes*. And the one who sang for him was
named Paiol.[5] And Bertran was a clever and a noble man.
And he called the Count of Brittany "Rassa"[6] and the King
of England "Oc e No,"[7] and the Young King, his son,
"Marinier."[8] And he had such a habit that he always stirred
up wars between the barons and embroiled the father and son
of England, until finally the Young King was killed by an
arrow in a castle of Bertran de Born.[9]

And Bertran de Born used to boast that he was of such
worth that he did not think he would ever need all his wit.
And afterwards the King took him prisoner, and after he had
imprisoned him, he said to him, "Bertran, you will now need
all of your wit." And Bertran answered that he had lost all
his wit when the Young King died. So the king wept for the
death of his son and pardoned him and gave him clothing and
land and honor. And he lived for a long time in this world
and later joined the order of Cîteaux.[10] And here you will
find some of his *sirventes*.

---

[1] Bertran was not from Limousin but from Perigord. The
    text of this vida, as opposed to the version of
    manuscript *A*, is fraught with errors.
[2] Bertran, we know, was not a viscount.
[3] Henry II (?).
[4] Alfonso II of Aragon (1162-11196) was a poet as well.
    He welcomed to his court many troubadours, among them
    Giraut de Borneil.
[5] More correctly, Papiol. Bertran's *tornadas* often
    refer to this jongleur.
[6] *Senhal* or code-name for Geoffrey of Brittany
    (1158-1196). (See Stimming, Nos. 4, 7, 10, 14, 28).
    Its meaning is "extortion," "conspiracy," "intrigue."
[7] *Senhal* for Richard the Lion-Hearted (1157-1199), not
    King Henry. The meaning of the phrase is "Yes and
    No."
[8] Although this *senhal* is for the Young King, Henry
    Court Mantel (1155-1183) (see Stimming, No. 28),
    Bertran uses it after Henry's death (see Stimming,
    Nos. 12, 24.) Its meaning is "Mariner."
[9] Henry Court Mantle did not die this way; he was taken
    ill in Martel (now in the arrondissement of Gourdon

[Lot]), where he later died.
[10] Bertran entered the abbey of Dalon, near Born, in
1197. He died there in 1215.

18. BERTRAN DE BORN THE YOUNGER

(Razo of P.-C. 81.1)

When King Richard died,[1] one of his brothers was left
whose name was Johans ses Terra[2] because he did not own any
portion of the land. And he was made King of England and he
had the kingdom, the duchy of Aquitaine, and the county of
Poitou.[3] And as soon as he was made king and lord of the
county and of the duchy of Poitou, he went to the Count of
Angoulême,[4] who had a very beautiful young daughter fifteen
years of age, and whom Lord Richard had betrothed to Lord
Ugo lo Brun, count of La Marche[5] and vassal and nephew of
Lord Jaufre de Lusignan.[6] And the Count of Angoulême had
promised him his daughter [for his wife] and received him as
a son, for he had no other sons or daughters. And John told
the Count of Angoulême that he wanted to marry his daughter
and made him give her to him; he married her right away, and
mounted his horse and went away with his wife to Normandy.

And when the Count of La Marche learned that the King had
taken his wife away from him, he was very sad and went to
complain to all his relatives and to all his friends, and
they were all very angry and deliberated whether to go to
Brittany and take the son of Count Geoffrey, who was called
Arthur,[7] and to make him their lord; for by right they
could do this, since he was the son of Count Geoffrey who
was born before King John. And thus they proceeded, and
made Arthur their lord and swore loyalty to him and led him
away to Poitou. And they took Poitou from the king, except
for a few castles and fortified villages which were there.
And King John lived with his wife in Normandy, so that
neither by day or night was he separated from her, whether
he was eating, or drinking, or sleeping or waking, and he

20

took her hunting with him in the forest and in the plains, with hawks and with falcons. And the barons took away all his land.

But it so happened that one day a great misfortune befell them, for they had beseiged the king's mother[8] in a castle called Mirabel.[9] Thanks to the help of another, John rescued her without anyone noticing and came to her so secretly that no one knew anything until he was inside the village with them. And he found them asleep and captured them all, Arthur and his barons and all those who were with him.

And because he was jealous of his wife, for he could not live without her, he abandoned Poitou and returned to Normandy, and left the prisoners [after] having them attest to oaths and give him hostages, and he crossed over to England. And he took with him Arthur and Lord Savaric de Mauléon[10] and the viscount of Châtellerault.[11] And he had his nephew Arthur drowned and had Lord Savaric de Mauléon put in the Corp tower,[12] where one never ate or drank, and the Viscount of Châtellerault likewise. And as soon as the King of France knew that King John had crossed over with his wife to England, he entered Normandy with a large army and took all his land. And the barons of Poitou revolted and took from him all of Poitou except La Rochelle.[13]

And Lord Savaric de Mauleon as a valiant, intelligent, and generous man, contrived to escape from prison, and took the castle in which he had been imprisoned. And King John made peace with Savaric, let him go, and entrusted to him all the land he had not lost in Poitou and in Gascony. And Lord Savaric went and started a war against all the enemies of King John, and took away from them all of Poitou and all of Gascony. And the king was enjoying himself in England in a room with his wife, and did not give Lord Savaric de Mauleon help or aid in money or in men. Lord Bertran de Born the Younger,[14] son of Lord Bertran de Born, the [author] of those other *sirventes*, on account of the needs of Lord Savaric de Mauleon and of the complaint that all the people of Aquitaine and the county of Poitou were making, wrote this *sirventes*:

When I see time renew itself.[15]

1 Richard the Lion-Hearted died in 1199.
2 Jean sans Terre, or John Lackland.
3 County bordered by Vendée and Limousin.
4 Aimar, Count of Angoulême. Angoulême is in
  Charente-Maritime.
5 Ugo IX of Lusignan, Count of La Marche, the region
  between Limousin and Combrailles, in the northwestern
  part of the Massif Central.
6 Lusignan is now seat of a canton in the arrondissement
  of Poitiers (Vienne). The Lusignan family used to own
  the county of La Marche.
7 The son of Geoffrey of Brittany was killed in 1203 by
  order of his uncle, King John Lackland.
8 Eleanor of Aquitaine.
9 Mirebeau-en-Poitou, in the arrondissement of Poitiers
  (Vienne).
10 Savaric de Mauléon, the troubadour, was seneschal of
  Poitou from 1200 to 1230. See Vida 93.
11 Guillaume de la Rochefoucauld.
12 According to Chabaneau, this is probably the chateau
  of Cardiff in Wales, on the Bristol canal. The
  castle was termed *Corp* by Latin chroniclers
  (*Biographies des troubadours*, p. 241, note 6).
13 La Rochelle was the ancient capital of Aunis; today
  it is the seat of the department of
  Charente-Maritime.
14 One of Bertran de Born's two sons, both of whom bore
  their father's name.
15 Cant vei lo temps renovelar (P.-C. 81.1)

19.   BERTRAN DEL POJET

   Bertran del Pojet[1] was a noble castellan from Provence,
from Teunes.[2] He was a valiant knight and generous, and a
good warrior. And he composed good songs and good
sirventes.

1 Puget is the seat of a canton in the arrondissement of

Nice (Alpes-Maritimes). Two songs survive; see C. de
Lollis, "Bertran del Pojet, trovatore dell'età
angioina", in *Miscellanea in onore di Arturo Graf*,
(Bergamo, 1903) p. 706ff.
[2] Region around Toulon (Var).

20. BLACASSET

Lord Blacasset was the son of Lord Blacatz,[1] who was the
best nobleman of Provence and the most honored baron and the
most able and the most generous and the most courtly and the
most gracious. And he was indeed his son in all merits, and
in all good deeds, and in all generosity. And he was a
great lover. And he took delight in inventing and was a
good inventor of poetry and composed many good songs.

[1] Blacasset was a Provençal lord, related to Raimon
Bérengar and to Charles of Anjou. He was not,
however, the son of Blacatz (see Vida 21), but one of
his distant relations. For his poems, see O. Klein,
Der Troubadour Blacassetz (Wiesbaden, 1887).

21. BLACATZ

Lord Blacatz[1] was from Provence, a noble baron,
high-born and rich, generous and clever. And he took
pleasure in gifts and gallantry and war and munificence and
courts and applause and noise and song and joy, and in all
those deeds by which a good man acquires fame and worth.
And there was never a man who took so much pleasure in

receiving as he did in giving. And he was one who supported
the abandoned and who gave refuge to the homeless. And as
time went by, he increased more in generosity and in
courtesy and in knightly valor and in lands and in rent and
in honor. And his friends loved him more, and his enemies
quarreled with him more. And he increased in wit and in
knowledge and in invention and in gaiety and in gallantry.

[1] The Blacas were a noble family related to the lords of
Baux. Blacatz was lord of Aups (today seat of a
canton in the arrondissement of Draguignan [Var]) and
a protector of troubadours. He is mentioned in many
poems. For further details, see O. Soltau, "Die Werke
des Trobadors Blacatz", *Zeitschrift für Romanische
Philologie*, *23* (1899), 201-248, and (*1900*), *33-60*;
Riquer, *Los Trovadores*, III, 1257-1260; Jeanroy,
Poésie lyrique, I, 177, note 1.

22. CADENET

Cadenet was from Provence, from a castle called
Cadenet,[1] which is on the bank of the Durance in the county
of Forcalquier.[2] He was the son of a poor knight. And when
he was a child, the castle of Cadenet was destroyed and
robbed by the people of the Count of Toulouse.[3] And the men
of the place were killed or taken prisoners. And he was
taken prisoner to the Toulousain[4] by a knight called
Guillem de Lantar.[5] And he brought him up and kept him in
his house. And he became good and handsome and courtly, and
he knew how to sing and how to talk well, and he learned how
to invent stanzas and *sirventes*.

And he took leave of the lord who had brought him up and
went around the courts and became a minstrel. And he had
himself called Baguas.[6] He traveled on foot for a long
time, miserable, around the world. And he came to Provence
and no one knew him. And he had himself called Cadenet and

he began to compose good and beautiful songs. And Lord Raimon Leugier de Dosfraires[7] from the bishopric of Nice provided him with equipment and honor. And Lord Blacatz[8] honored him and did him great good. For a long time he had great wealth and great honor. And later he entered the Hospital[9] and there he ended his days. And all his deeds I learned by listening and by seeing.

[1] Cadenet. Seat of a canton in the arrondissement of Apt (Vaucluse). The ruins of this castle still stand.

[2] Forcalquier is the seat of an arrondissement in Basses-Alpes. This county occupied most of the region of the Haute-Provence.

[3] Raimon V of Toulouse. According to Appel's edition of Cadenet's 23 poems (p. 6), this event took place between 1166 and 1176.

[4] Region around Toulouse, ancient *pagus Tholosanus*.

[5] Guillem Hunaud de Lantar, who died in 1222. Lantar is today Lanta, seat of a canton in the arrondissement of Toulouse.

[6] Masculine of *bagassa* ("prostitute"). It is unlikely that Cadenet would have given himself such a name; see Appel, *Der Trobador Cadenet*, p. 94, note 3. In any case, there are no extant poems from this period or under that name.

[7] Dosfraires was a castle in the county of Nice. Raimon's identity is unknown--he may have been related to a jongleur, Guillelm del Dui-Fraire, mentioned in a poem of Aimeric de Peguilhan.

[8] See Vida 21.

[9] Order of the Hospitalers, in Orange. See Vida of Raimbaut d'Aurenga (83), who is also said to have died here.

23. CASTELLOZA, NA

Lady Castelloza was from Auvergne, a noble lady, wife of Turc de Mairona.[1] And she loved Lord Arman de Brion[2] and composed songs about him. And she was a very gay and a very learned lady, and very beautiful. And here are written some of her songs.

[1] Probably one of the lords of the castle of Meyronne (commune of Venteuges, canton of Saugues, arrondissement of Le Puy [Haute-Loire].) Presumably the name *Turc* (meaning "Turk") recalls the valiant deeds of one of the Mairona family patriarchs who participated in a crusade around 1210 or 1220 (Boutière-Schutz, p. 334, note 2). For the three poems of Na Castelloza, see W. D. Paden, Jr. "The Poems of the *Trobairitz* Na Castelloza", *Romance Philology 35* (1981), 159-182; Schultz-Gora, p. 23 ff. and Bogin, pp. 118-129.

[2] A member of the house of Bréon. Bréon is today Brion, in the commune of Compains, canton of Besse-en-Chandesse, arrondissement of Issoire, Puy-de-Dôme.

24. CERCAMON

Cercamon[1] was a minstrel from Gascony, and he invented poems and pastorals in the old manner.[2] And he wandered all over the world wherever he could go, and for this reason he was called Cercamon.

[1] A professional pseudonym, derived from *cercar*, "to search, seek, go about," and *mon*, "world."

[2] *A la usanza antiga*, could possibly allude to Latin models; see E. Faral, "La Pastourelle," *Romania, 49* (1923), 241-242; E. Köhler, "Marcabrus *L'autrier*

jost'una sebissa und das Problem der Pastourelle,"
Romanistisches Jahrbuch, 5 (1952), 256-268. For
Cercamon's verses, see *The Poetry of Cercamon and
Jaufre Rudel*, ed. and trans. G. Wolf and R. Rosenstein
(New York, 1983) and A. Jeanroy, *Les Poésies de
Cercamon* (Paris, 1922) p. 29.

25. LO COMS DE RODES (THE COUNT OF RHODES)

(Razo of 185.3 and 457.33)

The Count of Rodez[1] was very able and very worthy, and
was also an inventor of poems. And Lord Uc de Saint Circ[2]
composed this couplet about him:

> Lord Count, you should not be ashamed
> For my sake, nor worry.
> For I have not come to you
> To look for or to ask for anything,
> For I possess all I need
> And I see that you lack money;
> For this reason I do not intend to ask for
> anything.
> If I gave to you, rather, I would be doing
> you a favor.[3]

The Count answered with this couplet:

> Lord Uc de Saint-Circ, I am sorry
> To see you, who this year were here,
> Poor and naked, deprived of everything,
> And who, thanks to me, returned a rich man.
> You cost me more than two archers
> Or two knights would cost,
> Yet I know well that if I gave you a palfrey
> God help me, you would gladly take it.[4]

27

[1] Ancient county; the modern city is seat of the department of Aveyron. No edition of the count's three surviving poems exists.

[2] See Vida 101.

[3] Seigner coms, no.us cal esmajar
Per mi, ni estar consiros,
Q'eu no sui ges vengutz a vos
Per [ren] querre ni demandar;
Qe ben ai so qe m'a mestier,
E vos vei qe fallon denier;
Per qe non ai en cor qe.us qera re;
Anz se.us dava, faria gran merce. (P.-C. 457.33)

[4] N'Uc de Sain Circ, be.m deu grevar
Q'e.us veja qe ojan sai fos
Paubres e nuz e d'aver blos,
Et eu fi vos en ric tornar;
Mais me costes qe dui arqier
No feiren o dui cavalier.
Pero ben sai, si.us dava un palafre,
Deus qe m'en gar, vos lo prendriatz be. (P.-C. 185.3)

26. LA COMTESSA DE DIA (THE COUNTESS OF DIA)

The Countess of Dia[1] was the wife of Lord Guillem de Poitou,[2] a beautiful and good lady. And she fell in love with Lord Raimbaut d'Aurenga[3] and composed many good songs about him.

[1] The identity of the earliest *trobairitz*, who probably lived in the late 12th century, continues to baffle scholars. Her works have been edited, without glossary or introduction, by G. Kussler-Ratyé, "Les chansons de la comtesse Béatrix de Dia," *Archivum Romanicum*, *1* (1917) 161-182; Bogin, pp. 82-91, provides texts and English translation; see also Jeanroy, *Poésie lyrique*, I, 170, note 9; 313-314. Die is the seat of an arrondissement in the department of Drôme.

[2] One of five possible persons. See Pattison, *The Life and Works of Raimbaut d'Orange*, (Minneapolis, 1952), pp. 29-30.

[3] According to Pattison (pp. 27-28) one of the great nephews of the troubadour Raimbaut d'Aurenga (Vida 83), called Raimbaut VI. He died in 1218.

27. DALFIN D'ALVERNHE (DAUPHIN OF AUVERGNE)

The Dalfin d'Alvernhe[1] was the Count of Auvergne, one of the wisest gentlemen and one of the most courtly and generous men in the world, and the best one at arms, the one who knew the most of love and of gallantry and of war and of all charming deeds. He was the most educated and the most creative, and the one who best invented *sirventes* and couplets and *tensos*, and the most able speaker ever, seriously as well as in jest. And because of his generosity, he lost half or more of his county. And by avarice and wisdom he knew how to recover it all, and to gain more than he had lost.

[1] Dauphin of Auvergne, son of Guilhem V, was prince of the house of Albon, born around 1150. He was Count of Clermont and Montferrand from 1168 to 1234. For details about his titles and parentage, see S. C. Aston, "The Name," pp. 140-163; Favati, p. 65, note 90. Although an article frequently precedes it, *Dalfin* (Dauphin) is a proper name and not a title. For Dalfin's ten poems, see E. M. Brackney, *A Critical Edition of the Poems of Dalfin d'Alvernhe* (Diss., University of Minnesota, 1937).

28. DAUDE DE PRADAS

Daude de Pradas[1] was from Rouergue from a town named Prades, four leagues from the city of Rodez, and he was canon of Maguelonne.[2] He was a wise man in letters, with natural wit and invention. And he was very knowledgeable about the nature of rapacious birds, and he composed songs through a sense of invention, but they were not inspired by love; for this reason they were not pleasing to the people, and were not sung.

[1] Prades-Salars is in the canton of Pont-de-Salars, arrondissement of Rodez, Aveyron. For Daude de Pradas' nineteen poems, see A. H. Schutz, *Poésies de Daude de Pradas* (Toulouse, 1933).

[2] In the Hérault. Although a certain Deodatus de Pratis appears as canon in the archives of Aveyron in 1242, it is not likely that the troubadour Daude de Prades was a canon; see Boutière-Schutz, p. 234, note 2.

29. ELIAS DE BARJOLS

Lord Elias de Barjols[1] was from Agenais,[2] from a castle called Pérols.[3] He was the son of a merchant. And he sang better than any other man who lived at that time. And he became a minstrel, and he was accompanied by another minstrel called Oliver,[4] and they went around the courts together for a long time. And the Count Anfos of Provence[5] kept them with him, and gave them wives and land in Barjols, and for this reason they were called Lord Elias and Oliver de Barjols.

And Lord Elias fell in love with the Countess, Milady Garsenda,[6] wife of the count, after Anfos died in Sicily,[7] and composed about her his beautiful and good songs, for as long as she lived. And he entered the Hospital of Saint

Beneic[8] of Avignon, and there he died. And he composed the songs which are written here.

[1] Barjols is today the seat of a canton in the arrondissement of Draguignan, Var.
[2] Region of Agen in Guyenne.
[3] Pérols-sur-Vézère, in the arrondissement of Tulle (Corrèze). See Boutière-Schutz, p. 216, note 1.
[4] Unknown.
[5] Alfonse II, son of Alfonso II of Aragon and brother of Pierre II, governed Provence for his brother from 1185 to 1196, and alone until his death in 1209.
[6] Garsenda of Sabran or of Forcalquier was the daughter of Guillaume IV, last count of Forcalquier. She married Alfonse II in 1193 and was the mother of Raimon-Bérengar IV (1209-1245). Elias mentions her in several songs: S. Stronski, *Le Troubadour Elias de Barjols* (Toulouse, 1906), nos. 5, 6, 7 and 8.
[7] Alfonse II died in Perpignan.
[8] Hospital of the "frères Pontifes," founded in Avignon by Bénézet.

30. ELIAS CAIREL

A. Version of manuscripts *AIK*

Elias Cairel[1] was from Sarlat,[2] a town in Perigord, and was a craftsman of gold and silver and a draughtsman of arms. And he became a minstrel and traveled for a long time around the world. He sang badly, and invented poetry badly, and played the fiddle badly, and spoke still more badly, but he wrote words and melodies very well. He was in Romania[3] for a long time. And when he left there, he returned to Sarlat, and there he died.

[1] Elias Cairel's fourteen works were edited by H. Jaeschke, *Der Trobador Elias Cairel* (Berlin, 1921).

[2] Seat of an arrondissement in Dordogne.
[3] The Byzantine Empire.

B. Version of manuscript *H*

Elias Cairel was from Perigord, and he was well versed in letters and very clever at inventing poetry and at everything he wanted to do or say. And he visited most of the inhabited parts of the world. And because of his disdain for the barons and the times, he was not as esteemed as his work merited.

31. ELIAS FONSALADA

Lord Elias Fonsalada was from Bergerac,[1] from the bishopric of Perigord. He was a very handsome man in appearance, and he was the son of a burgher who became a minstrel; and Lord Elias was also a minstrel. He was not a good inventor of poetry, but rather a storyteller,[2] and he knew how to behave well in society.

[1] Seat of an arrondissement in Dordogne.
[2] Boutière and Schutz interpret *noellaire* as "auteur d'un genre particulier" or "un beau parleur" (p. 235). I follow Levy's definition of *novelador*, "auteur de nouvelles." See M. Raupach, p. 141, note 2.

32. FERRARI DA FERRARA

Master Ferrari[1] was from Ferrara. And he was a minstrel and he understood better how to invent poems in Provençal than any other man who ever was in Lombardy, and he was the one who best understood the Provençal language. And he was well versed in letters and wrote better than anyone in the world, and he composed many good and beautiful books.

He was a courtly man in person, and a good man. He always served the barons and the knights gladly. And he always stayed at the house of the Estes. And when it happened that the marquis held feasts and court, and the minstrels came who understood the Provençal language, they all went to him and called him their master. And if anyone came who understood better than the others and asked questions about his invention or something else, Master Ferrari would answer him at once. So that he was like a champion in the court of the Marquis of Este.

But he never composed more than two songs and one *retroensa*.[2] However, he also composed many of the best *sirventes* and couplets in the world. And he compiled an anthology of all the songs of the good troubadours of the world, and from each song or *sirventes* he extracted one or two or three couplets, those which carry the meanings of the songs and in which all the words are distinct. And this anthology is written in here. And in this anthology he did not intend to place any of his own couplets, but the owner of the book had them written in so that he Ferrari would be remembered.

And Master Ferrari loved a lady called Milady Turcla[3] when he was young. And he performed many good deeds for this lady. And when he became old, he did not travel much except to go to Treviso to [see] Milord Giraut de Chamin[4] and his sons. And they bestowed great honor upon him and saw him gladly, and they welcomed him well and gladly gave him gifts because of his goodness and because of their love for the Marquis of Este.

[1] Probably Ferrarino Trogni da Ferrara, a notary.
[2] Only one *cobla* of Ferrari has been preserved (P.-C. 229.1/50.1). *Retronchas* (see Glossary) are also

attributed to Raimon de las Salas (Vida 88).

[3] A lady from the house of Turcli;see Bertoni, *Trovatori*, p. 128.

[4] Girardo III da Camino (d. 1307), mentioned by Dante in *Purgatorio* 16.124-140 as "buon Gherardo." The Da Camino family was close to the Este family (Jeanroy, *Poésie Lyrique*, I, 259.)

33. FOLQUET DE MARSEILLA (OF MARSEILLE)

Folquet of Marseille[1] was the son of a merchant from Genoa who was called Sir Anfos. And when the father died, he left Folquet very wealthy. Then Folquet sought fame and merit. And he began to serve the worthy barons and the worthy men and to frequent them, and to give, and to serve, and to come, and to go. And he was greatly esteemed and honored by King Richard[2] and by the count Raimon of Toulouse[3] and by Lord Baral, his lord from Marseille.[4]

He invented poetry very well, and was a very charming man in appearance. And he loved the wife of his lord, Lord Baral. And he wooed her and composed his songs about her. But neither by his requests nor by his songs did he ever find her grace, that she would grant him any of love's favors. For this reason he always complains about Love in his songs. And it so happened that the lady died and Lord Baral, her husband and his lord, who honored him so, died too. And so did the good King Richard, the good Count Raimon of Toulouse, and King Anfos of Aragon.[5]

Because of his sadness over [the death] of his lady and the princes I told you about, he abandoned the world. And he joined the order of Citeaux with his wife and his two sons. And so he was made abbot of a rich abbey which is in Provence, and which is called Torondet.[6] And later he was made Bishop of Toulouse.[7] And there he died.

[1] Folquet is the diminutive of Folc. Fulco Anfos

34

appears in a document of 1178 listing various bourgeois of Marseille. Anfos was the name of a well-known Genoese family.

[2] Richard the Lion-Hearted (d. 1199) is mentioned in several of Folquet's poems. See S. Stronski, *Le Troubadour Folquet de Marseille* (Krakow, 1910), pp. 87 ff., 142.

[3] Raimon V (d. 1194).

[4] Raimon Gaufredi Barral, on whose death (1192) Folquet composed a *planh* (lament).

[5] Alfonso II (1162-1196), mentioned in Stronski, p. 83.

[6] Folquet, his wife, and sons entered Le Thoronet (diocese of Fréjus [Var]) in 1200; Folquet became abbot shortly thereafter.

[7] Folquet was Bishop of Toulouse from 1206 until his death in 1231. Dante, regarded Folquet as a saint and gave him an important role in *Paradiso* 9.

34. FOLQUET DE ROMANS

Folquet de Romans[1] was from Viennois[2] from a town called Romans.[3] He was a good minstrel, who was well at ease in the courts and of pleasant conversation. And he was well honored among high society. And he composed *sirventes* in the manner of the jongleurs[4] to praise the good and to blame the bad.

[1] Folquet de Romans' poems were edited by R. Zenker: *Die Gedichte des Folquet von Romans*, (Halle, 1896).

[2] Region around Vienne (Isère).

[3] Romans is the seat of a canton in the arrondissement of Valence (Drôme).

[4] The text gives *sirventes joglarescs*. See Mejean, "Contribution".

35. GARIN D'APCHIER

Garin d'Apchier[1] was a noble castellan from Gevaudan,[2] from the bishopric of Mende,[3] which is on the border of Auvergne and of Rouergue,[4] and of the bishopric of Puy Sainta Maria.[5] He was a valiant and good warrior, and generous and a good inventor of poems, and a handsome knight. And he knew all there was to know about love and gallantry. And he composed the first *descort* which begins:

When the leaf and the flower bud
and I hear the song of the nightingale.[6]

[1] Apcher is in the commune of Prunières, arrondissement of Marvejols (Lozère).
[2] Ancient region of the *Gabales* whose capital was *Gavalis*, today Javols (Lozère).
[3] Seat of the department of Lozère.
[4] Today the department of Aveyron.
[5] Puy-Sainte-Marie or Le Puy-en-Velay (Haute-Loire).
[6] Quan foill'e flors reverdezis
Et aug lo chan del rossignol. (P.-C. 162.6)
These are the only extant verses of Garin d'Apchier; see C. Appel, "Poésies provençales inédites tirées des manuscrits d'Italie", *Revue des Langues Romanes*, *34* (1890), 12.

36. GARIN LO BRUN

Garin lo Brun was a noble lord of the manor of Velay in the bishopric of Puy Sainta Maria,[1] and he was a good inventor of poetry, and he went to the trouble of telling the ladies how they should behave themselves. He was not a composer of poems, nor of songs, but of *tensos*.[2]

36

[1] Le Puy-en-Velay (Haute-Loire).
[2] See C. Appel, "L'Enseignement de Garin lo Brun", *Revue des Langues Romanes*, *33* (1889), 404-32, for the text of this *tenso*.

37. GAUCELM FAIDIT

Gaucelm Faidit[1] was from a town called Uzerche,[2] which is in the bishopric of Limousin, and he was the son of a burgher. And he sang worse than anyone in the world, but he composed many good melodies and good rhymes. And he became a minstrel because he lost all his belongings in a game of dice. He was a man of great girth, and he exhibited great gluttony in eating and drinking. This is why he became extraordinarily fat. For a long time he was very unhappy, receiving neither presents nor honor. For more than twenty years he wandered on foot around the world, for neither he nor his songs were esteemed or wanted.

And he married a prostitute[3] whom he took with him around the courts, and her name was Guillelma Monja.[4] She was extremely beautiful and extremely learned, and she became as large and as fat as he was. And she was from a rich town called Alais[5] in the march of Provence under the suzerainty of Lord Bernart d'Anduze.[6] And my lord the Marquis Bonifacis de Monferrat[7] gave him wealth and clothing, and granted distinction to him and to his songs.

[1] Gaucelm Faidit's 65 poems have been edited by J. D. Mouzat: *Les Poèmes de Gaucelm Faidit, troubadour du XIIe siècle* (Paris, 1965). Part of this vida was translated by Pound in "Troubadours--Their Sorts and Conditions," *Literary Essays*, p. 99.
[2] Seat of a canton in the arrondissement of Tulle (Corrèze).
[3] The text gives *soldadera*. According to Raynouard and Levy, *soudadieira* means "prostitute." Bergin points out that *soldadera* was the name given to a woman who

performed with jongleurs (*Anthology*, II, 44).

[4] Probable pun: *monja* means "nun."

[5] In the department of Gard.

[6] Probably Bernard VII of Anduze (Gard), who died around 1223.

[7] Boniface II, who in 1192 suceeded his father Guillaume III, was chosen in 1202 to lead the Fourth Crusade. He died in 1207. Gaucelm celebrated the marquis in at least six of his songs and also followed him to the crusade.

38. GAUSBERT AMIEL

Gaubert[1] Amiel was from Gascony, a poor knight, courtly and skilled at arms. He knew how to invent poetry and never courted a lady more noble than he. And he composed his poems with more measure than any other person who ever invented them.

[1] Or Gausbert. No works remain.

39. GAUSBERT DE POICIBOT (JAUSBERT DE PUYCIBOT)

The monk Gausbert de Poicibot[1] was a noble man from the bishopric of Limoges, son of a castellan of Poicibot. And he was put into holy orders when he was a child, in a monastery called Saint Lunart.[2] And he was well versed in letters and knew how to sing and how to invent poetry well.

And desiring a woman, he left the monastery and went to
the one to whom all those who wished honor and kindness in
exchange for courtesy came, Lord Savaric de Mauleon.[3] And
he gave him a minstrel's equipment, clothing, and horses.
So he then went around the courts and invented and wrote
good songs.

And he fell in love with a noble and beautiful damsel and
composed his songs about her. And she did not want to love
him unless he became a knight and married her. And he told
Lord Savaric how the lady refused him. So Lord Savaric
knighted him and gave him land and rent, and he took the
damsel for his wife and greatly honored her.

And then it happened that he went to Spain, and the
damsel stayed. And a knight from England fell in love with
her and did and said so much that he managed to take her
away and had her for a long time as his mistress, and then
he abandoned her in a wicked way.

And when Gausbert returned from Spain, he stayed for an
evening in the city where she was. And when evening came,
he went out desiring a woman and entered the dwelling of a
poor woman, for he had been told that there was a beautiful
damsel inside. And he came upon his own wife. And when he
saw her, and she saw him, they both felt great pain and
great shame. He stayed with her that night, and the
following morning he left with her and took her to a
convent, which he made her enter. And because of this pain,
he stopped inventing poems and singing. And here are some
of his songs.

[1] Poicibot is not a known place. The fifteen poems of
Gausbert were edited by W. P. Shepard, *Les Poésies de
Jausbert de Puycibot, troubadour du XIIIe siècle*
(Paris, 1924). This vida is cited by Pound in
"Troubadours-- Their Sorts and Conditions," *Literary
Essays*, pp. 95-96, and Gausbert appears in Canto 5.
[2] Saint-Léonard-des-Chaumes, near La Rochelle.
[3] See Vida 93; Shepard, *Poésies*, p. iv.

39

40. GAUSERAN DE SAINT LEIDIER

Gauseran de San Leidier[1] was from the bishopric of
Velay, a noble castellan, son of the daughter of Guilhem de
San Leidier.[2] And he fell in love with the Countess of
Viennois,[3] daughter of the Marquis Guillem de Monferrat.

[1] Saint-Didier-la-Séauve is in the arrondissement of
Yssingeaux (Haute-Loire). The first name is also
spelled Gauceran. Two poems survive, but have not
been edited.
[2] See Vida 47.
[3] Countess Béatrice de Montferrat was the daughter of
Guillem IV; in 1220 she married the Dauphin of Vienne,
André d'Albon. Viennois is the region around Vienne
(Isère).

41. GIRAUT DE BORNEILL

Giraut de Borneill[1] was from Limousin, from the region
of Excideuil,[2] from a rich castle belonging to the viscount
of Limoges. And he was a man of low birth, but he was
intelligent in letters and had a natural wit. And he was
the best inventor of poetry among any of the ones who came
before him or who came after him. For this reason he was
called the master of the inventors and he is still so called
by all those who truly understand subtle discourse in which
love and reason are well expressed. He was greatly honored
by the worthy men and by those who understood love, and by
the ladies who understood the masterly words of his songs.

And his life was such that all winter he spent in school,
and he taught[3] letters, and all summer he traveled about
the courts and took with him two singers who sang his songs.
He never wanted a wife, and everything he earned he gave to
his poor relatives and to the church of the village where he

was born. This church was called, and still is, Saint
Gervais. And here are written a great number of his songs.

[1] Borneill, according to Chabaneau, is probable Bourneix
in the canton of Lanouaille, arrondissement of
Nontron, near Excideuil (*Biographies*, p. 352, note 1.)
Sometimes spelled Bornelh.
[2] In the arrondissement of Périgueux (Dórdogne).
[3] Here *aprender* means "teach" rather than "learn"; A.
Kolsen, *Sämtliche Lieder des Trobadors Giraut de
Bornelh* (Halle, 1910-1935) II, 78. For a later
edition of the 76 poems, see B. Panvini, *Giraldo di
Bornelh, trovatore del sec. XII* (Catania, 1949).

42. GIRAUT DE CALANSO

Guiraut de Calanso[1] was a minstrel from Gascony. He was
well versed in letters and was clever at inventing poetry,
and he composed skillful songs, *desplazens*[2] and *descortz*
[as were written] at that time. He and his words were
disliked in Provence, and he enjoyed little honor among
courtly society.

[1] Either Calanso, in Gascony (?), or Chalançon, in the
arrondissement of Tournon (Ardèche) or in the
arrondissement of Die (Drôme).
[2] A kind of verse composition (see Glossary). Boutière
and Schutz read the phrase differently, making
desplazens an adjective. Their version thus reads:
"il fit des chansons composées avec art, mais de ton
déplaisant" ["he composed skillful songs of a
displeasing tone"] (p. 217). For Giraut de Calanso's
eleven poems, see W. Ernst, "Die Lieder des
provenzalischen Trobadors Guiraut von Calanso,"
Romanische Forschungen, 44 (1930), 255-406. See also
F. Goldin, *The Mirror of Narcissus* (Ithaca, 1967), pp.
71-81 for discussion of Giraut's concept of love.

43. GIRAUT DE SALIGNAC

Giraut de Salignac was from Quercy,[1] from the castle of Salignac.[2] He was a minstrel. He was a very able man and very courtly, and he invented songs and *descortz* and *sirventes* with grace and skill.

[1] Region around Cahors, in the department of Lot.
[2] In the arrondissement of Sarlat, Dordogne.

44. GUI DE CAVAILLO(N)

Gui de Cavaillon was a noble baron of Provence, lord of Cavaillon.[1] He was a generous and courtly man, and a charming knight, and was greatly loved by the ladies and by all the people. He was a capable knight and a good warrior. And he composed good *tensos* and good couplets about love and about conversations.[2] And he was believed to be the lover of Countess Garsenda,[3] wife of the Count of Provence, who was a brother of the King of Aragon.[4] And he sent these couplets to Lord Bertran Folcon:[5]

I will compose two couplets for this melody
Which I will send to Lord Bertran
                              d'Avignon.
Let him know that I am in Castel-Nou
And that the French are surrounding us.
I remember well her to whom I belong
For I often dig in my spurs, shout my war cry
And display the lion on my shield.
This is why I am sending it to Bertran
                              d'Avignon
          Yes, to Bertran!
To Bertran Folc I send this as an imprisoned
                              man--
That he may be willing to come here--
For during the day we are armed on horseback
And later, in the evening, as soon as we have

42

                                          all dined,
We keep watch between the wall and the moat. ·
And with the French there is no truce,
Instead countless blows are being exchanged.
And this has gone on for well over three
                                          months,
But he has just stayed there calmly--
And then he left without taking leave of us,
          Bertran Folcon.[6]

[1] The name of Gui de Cavaillo or Cavaillon appears in
    many documents from 1205 to 1224 but his six works
    have not yet been edited. He fought in Provence
    (1216-17) and was advisor to Raimon-Bérengar; see
    Jeanroy, *Poésie Lyrique*, I, 179-180. Cavaillon is in
    the arrondissement of Avignon (Vaucluse).
[2] The text gives *coblas de solatz*. Boutière and Schutz
    hesitate in translating "couplets. . .plaisants" (p.
    506) and "*coblas* humoristiques" (p. 507). Bergin, on
    the other hand, renders the phrase "*tenso*" (*Anthology*,
    II, 228).
[3] Garsende of Sabran or of Forcalquier, daughter of
    Guillaume IV, last Count of Forcalquier
    (Basses-Alpes). She was the wife of Alfonse II and
    mother of Raimon-Bérengar IV (1209-1245). She was
    celebrated by the troubadour Elias de Barjols (see
    Vida 29).
[4] Alphonse II of Provence was the brother of Pedro II of
    Aragon.
[5] Bertran Folcon of Avignon, sometimes confused with
    Bertran d'Avignon, also a poet. See Boutière-Schutz,
    p. 507, note 4, and S. Guida, "Per la biografia", pp.
    189-210.
[6] Doas coblas farai en aqest son,
    Q'eu trametrai a 'N Bertram d'Avignon.
    E sapça be qe dinz Castel-Nou son,
    E li Franceis nos estan d'eviron.
    E membra.m be de cela cui hom son:
    Qe sovendet en broc e.n esperon,
    E crit m'enseigna e desplec mon leon.
    Per q'eu o man a Bertram d'Avignon,
          Hoc, a 'N Bertram!
    A 'N Bertram Folc man, com hom esserat,

Per zo q'el aia del venir volontat,
Q'el jorn estam nos el caval armat,
E puois, al vespre, can tost avem sopat,
Nos fam la gaita entre.l mur e.l fossat;
Et ab franceis non a.n ges entregat,
Enanz i son mainz colps pres e donat,
Et [d']aizo a[ja] be tres mes passat,
Et el i a tot soau sojornat,
Pois se parti de nos se[ne]s comjat
         Bertram Folcon. (P.-C. 192.2)

45. GUI D'UISEL

   Gui d'Uisel was from Limousin, a noble castellan, and he
and his brothers and his cousin Lord Elias were lords of
Ussel,[1] which is a rich castle. And his two brothers were
called Lord Ebles and Lord Elias. And the four of them were
composers of poetry. Gui used to invent good songs, and
Lord Elias good *tensos*, and Lord Ebles bad *tensos*, and Lord
Peire expressed in song everything that the three invented.
Lord Gui was Canon of Brioude[2] and Montferrand,[3] and for a
long time he loved Lady Margarita d'Aubusson[4] and the
Countess of Montferrand,[5] about whom he composed many good
songs. But the papal legate[6] made him swear never to
compose songs again. And for this reason he stopped
inventing and singing.

   [1] Ussel-sur-Sarzonne is the seat of an arrondissement in
       Corrèze. See J. Audiau, *Les Poésies des quatre
       troubadours d'Ussel* (Paris, 1922).
   [2] Seat of an arrondissement in the Haute-Loire.
   [3] In Puy-de-Dôme.
   [4] Wife of viscount Rainaut VI of Aubusson (1201-1245).
       Aubusson is the seat of an arrondissement in Creuse.
   [5] Wife of Robert I, Dauphin of Auvergne.
   [6] Pierre de Castelnau, legate of Pope Innocent III.
       Gui's renunciation of poetry may be dated before 1209.

In 1214 the Council of Montpellier forbade mingling of clerics with *curias vel hospicia vel colloquia mulierum* (Boutière-Schutz, p. 204).

46. GUILLEM IX, LO COMS DE PEITIEUS
(WILLIAM IX, THE COUNT OF POITIERS)

The Count of Poitiers[1] was one of the most courtly men in the world, and one of the greatest deceivers of women, a very capable knight and very liberal in gallantry. And he knew how to invent poetry and how to sing very well, and he wandered around the world in order to deceive the ladies. And he had a son whose wife was the Duchess of Normandy,[2] who had a daughter who was the wife of King Henry of England[3] and the mother of the Young King[4] and of Richard,[5] and of Count Geoffrey of Brittany.[6]

[1] Ancient capital of the province of Poitou, today seat of the department of Vienne. The man is William IX, Duke of Aquitaine, Count VII of Poitou (Poitiers).

[2] The vida is not accurate on this point. William X, the poet's son, married Aénor of Châtellerault. It was their daughter, Eleanor of Aquitaine, who became duchess of Normandy when she married Henry II of England in 1152. Details of this troubadour's life, surprisingly absent from the vida, are provided by Gerald A. Bond, *The Poetry of William VII*, *Count of Poitiers*, *IX Duke of Aquitaine* (New York: 1982) pp. xiv-xlix; see this latest edition also for Guillem's eleven poems. See also Pound, Canto 6.

[3] Henry Plantagenet, later Henry II (1154-1189).

[4] Henry Courtmantle (1158-1183), crowned in 1170.

[5] Richard I the Lion-Hearted (1157-1199), King of England from 1189 to 1199.

[6] Geoffrey of Brittany (1158-1186).

47. GUILLEM ADEMAR

Guillem Ademar was from Gevaudan,[1] from a castle named
Meyrueis.[2] He was a noble man, son of a poor knight. And
the lord of Meyrueis made him a knight. And was a very
worthy man, eloquent, and he knew well how to invent
poetry.[3] And he was unable to support his rank as a knight,
and he became a minstrel. And he was greatly honored by all
the high society. And later he joined the order of
Grandmont.[4]

[1] Ancient region of *Gabales*, today Javols (Lozère).
[2] In the arrondissement of Florac (Lozère).
[3] For his poems, see K. Almquist, *Poésies du troubadour
Guillem Ademar* (Uppsala, 1951).
[4] Grandmont is a Benedictine abbey near Limoges (commune
of Saint-Sylvestre, canton of Laurière.)

48. GUILLEM AUGIER NOVELLA

Ogier[1] was a minstrel from Viennois,[2] and he spent a
long time in Lombardy. And he composed good *descortz* and
sirventes in the manner of jongleurs,[3] in which he praised
some and blamed others.

[1] Augier Novella. His name is spelled diversely in the
manuscripts.
[2] The poet was born in Saint-Donat-en-Viennois, in the
arrondissement of Valence (Drôme). Other details in
this vida are historically accurate; for a discussion
of the biography and texts of the poems see J. Müller,
"Die Gedichte des Guillem Augier Novella," *Zeitschrift
für Romanische Philologie*, *27* (1903), 48 ff.
[3] The text gives *sirventes joglarescs*. A definition of
this genre, which also appears in Vidas 66 and 34, is
provided by S. Mejean, "Contribution".

49.   GUILLEM DE BALAUN

(Version of manuscript *H*. *Razo of P.-C. 208.1*.)

Guillem de Balaun[1] was a noble castellan from the region
of Montpellier,[2] very able and learned and a good inventor
of poetry. And he fell in love with a noble lady from the
bishopric of Gevaudan,[3] whose name was Milady Guilelma de
Jau[j]ac,[4] wife of Lord Peire, lord of Jaujac. He loved
her very much and served her and honored her by talking and
singing. And the lady loved him so much that she did and
said everything that pleased him in the matter of love.

Lord Guillem had a companion named Peire de Barjac,[5] who
was worthy and valiant and good and handsome. And he loved
in the castle of Jaujac a lady, young and beautiful, named
Milady Vierneta.[6] And she had kept him as her knight and he
received from her everything he wanted. Both of them were
lovers of their ladies, Guillem de Balaun and Peire de
Barjac.

And it so happened that Peire de Barjac quarreled with
his lady, so that she dismissed him in a bad way. So he
left, grieving and sadder than he had ever been. And
Guillem de Balaun consoled him much, [telling him] not to
despair, for he would reconcile him to his lady as soon as
he returned to Jaujac. It was a long time before he
returned there. And as soon as Guillem de Balaun returned
to Jaujac, he reconciled Milady Vierneta and Lord Peire de
Barjac. So he felt more joy than he had ever felt before.
Guillem de Balaun was very amazed when he heard Peire de
Barjac say that he had never been rendered so happy by any
joy, not even when he had first won his lady.

So Guillem de Balaun said he wanted to test whether the
joy of recovering a lady's love was as great as the joy of
first winning her. And he pretended to be very angry with
Milady Guilelma. And he did not send her any messages, nor
talk about her, nor hear her being talked about, nor did he
wish to go to the region where she lived. So she sent him
her messenger with very loving letters, wondering why he had
been so long without seeing her or without sending her any
messages. And he, like a foolish lover, did not want to
hear or to listen to the messenger or the letters, and had

him expelled from the castle with shame. The messenger
returned, grieving and sad, to my lady Guilelma and told her
the news. So she was very sad and ordered a knight from her
castle who knew about their affair to go to Lord Guillem de
Balaun and ask him why he was angry with her, and if she had
done or said anything which displeased him. For she wished
to make amends as he saw best and as he wished.

The knight went to Balaun, and Lord Guillem saw him and
received him badly. And when he had told him what my lady
Guilelma had sent him to say, Guillem answered that he would
not tell him the reason [for his anger], for she knew well
that the motive was such that it could not be amended and
that it could not be pardoned. The knight returned and told
Milady Guilelma what Lord Guillem had said. So she became
desperate and said that she would never send him a messenger
again, nor ever plea nor excuse [him again]. Thus the lady
spent a long time in great sadness. Lord Guillem started to
think how he was losing great joy and great happiness
because of his folly.

And so he mounted his horse and went to Jaujac. And he
stayed at the house of a burgher and not in the court,
saying that he was going on a pilgrimage. And when the
night came, when people were in bed, Milady Guilelma left
the castle with a lady and a damsel, and came to the house
where he lay. And she asked for the lady of the house and
asked to be led to the room in which Guillem lay. And she
came to the bed where he was and fell on her knees in front
of him. And she lowered her veil to kiss him, asking him
pardon for whatever wrong she had done. And he did not want
to receive her, nor pardon the wrong she had done him.
Rather, beating and hitting her, he drove her out of his
presence. And the lady went away, sad and ill-disposed and
grieving, to her house, resolved never to see him nor to
talk to him, and sorry for what Love had made her do.

And Guillem likewise remained grieving because of what
folly had made him do. And he arose in the course of time
and came to the castle and made it known that he wished to
see my lady Guilelma, for he wished to show her and to tell
her about the follies he had done and why he had done them.
And he wished to get her to pardon his folly. And the lady
did not want to see him or hear him. Rather she ordered him
to leave and had him thrown out of the castle. And he left

like a madman and a fool, lamenting and weeping and sighing. And the lady remained repentant of the submission she had shown him.

In this manner Guillem de Balaun spent over a year, for the lady did not ever want to see him or to hear him talked about by anyone who wanted to do so. So he composed the desperate poem which says:

Begging your forgiveness,
        I send you this poem. [7]

And Lord Bernart d'Anduze, [8] who was the most honored baron of that region and was a friend of Guillem and of Milady Guilelma, took her the written poem. And he asked her most insistently to grant him this favor of pardoning him and of first of all taking revenge of him. And she said that, since he insisted so, she would take vengeance and pardon him. But she wanted the revenge to be this: that Lord Guillem should pull out the fingernail of the longest finger and bring it to her.

Bernart d'Anduze returned to Lord Guillem and told him of the revenge she wanted and of the pardon she would grant him. And he was the happiest man in the world. And at once he had his finger tied and the nail pulled out. And he mounted his horse with Lord Bernart d'Anduze and went to Milady Guilelma, at Jaujac. And they both fell at her feet, begging her pardon. And he presented her with his fingernail. And she received it and so pardoned his ignorant folly. And it is just that a man who has great good and seeks his own unhappiness should find it, as did Guillem de Balaun. For thus a foolish man chastises himself: by suffering harm.

---

[1] Balaun is probably Balazuc, in the commune of Vallon, arrondissement of Largentière (Ardèche). This troubadour's extant poems have been edited by J. Boutière in "Le troubadour Guillem de Balaun," *Annales du Midi, 48* (1948), p. 228.

[2] Seat of the department of Hérault.

[3] Ancient region of *Gabales*, today the department of Lozère.

[4] Jaujac (old *Gaudiacum*) is now a commune in the canton

of Thueyts, arrondissement of Largentière (Ardèche).
⁵ See Vida 68. Barjac is a commune in the
arrondissement of Alès (Gard).
⁶ Unknown lady. According to Favati (p. 510), this
could be Vierna d'Anduze, wife of Raimon I, Baron of
Gauges (Hérault).
⁷ Lo vers mou mercejan vas vos. (P.-C. 208.1)
⁸ Probably Bernard VII of Anduze (Gard), who died in
1223.

50.   GUILLEM DEL BAUS

(Razo of P.-C. 392.31)

Guilelm des Baux,[1] Prince of Orange,[2] robbed a merchant
of France and took great wealth from him as he went on his
route.   And the merchant went to appeal to the King of
France.[3]   And the king told him that he could not do justice
for him because it had taken place too far away.   "But I
give you my word that in whatever way you can help yourself,
you may do it."

And the burgher went and counterfeited the king's seal.
And he had letters forged from the king to Lord Guilelm del
Baux, asking him to come to the king and promising him great
wealth, great honors, and great gifts.   And when Guilelm des
Baux received the letters, he rejoiced much and made great
preparations to go to the king.   And he started out and came
to the city of the merchant whom he had robbed; for he did
not know where he could be.   And the burgher, when he knew
that Lord Guilelm was in the city, had him seized and
apprehended his companions.   And so he made him return
everything he had taken from him and had him make amends for
all the damage.

And Guilelm returned poor and destitute.   And he was
going to take[4] some land of Lord Aimar of Poitiers[5] called
the Osteilla.[6]   And as he was coming on the Rhône in a small

boat, he was seized by the fishermen of Lord Aimar. Lord Raimbaut de Vaqueiras, who called himself and Guillem "Engles,"[7] composed these couplets about this matter:

Everyone asks me, Engles, to reproach you
For the mad journey from which you have
                                foolishly returned.
Any other than you would have been ruined,
But you possess such a noble and exalted heart
That you can hide the madness which no man
                                can pardon.
And had the people of Estella been French,
They would have taken revenge.
For they reproach the king for not having
                                done so.[8]

---

[1] Guillaume IV was the son of Bertran des Baux and of a sister of Raimbaut d'Aurenga (see Vida 83). Les Baux is in the canton of Saint-Rémy, arrondissement of Arles (Bouches-du-Rhône).

[2] In the arrondissement of Avignon (Vaucluse).

[3] Philippe-Auguste (1180-1223).

[4] *Presar*, Boutière-Schutz translate "piller(?)" (p. 486).

[5] Ademar II, count of Diois or of Valentinois (1181-1230), wrote a *partimen* with Raimbaut de Vaqueiras and Perdigon.

[6] Unknown place.

[7] *Senhal* which appears in several of Raimbaut de Vaqueiras' (see Vida 84) poems but does not seem to designate the same person every time. See Linskill, *The Poems of R. de Vaqueiras* (The Hague, 1964), pp. 27-28.

[8] [T]uit me pregon, Engles, q'eu vos don saut
Del fol anar ond es e[n] fol[s] vengutz,
Don totz autr' om fora decasegutz;
Mas vos es tant de ric coratg' e d'aut
Qe la foudat, dont nuls hom no.us rasona,
Sabetz cobrir; e si foson Frances
Cil d'Estella, venjamen n'agra[n] pres,
Car no.us donet lo reis, c'om n'ochaiçona. (P.-C. 392.31)

51

51. GUILLEM DE BERGUEDAN

Guillem de Berguedan was a noble baron of Catalonia,[1] viscount of Berguedan,[2] lord of Madorna[3] and of Riechs,[4] a good knight and a good warrior. And he waged a great war against Raimon Folc de Cardona,[5] who was richer and greater than he. And it so happened that one day he came upon Raimon Folc, and he killed him in a bad way. And because of the death of Lord Raimon Folc, he was dispossessed. For a long time he was supported by his relatives and his friends, but later they all abandoned him except Lord Arnaut de Castelbon,[6] who was a worthy man of that region, noble and great. He composed good *sirventes*, in which he slandered some and praised others, and he boasted of all the ladies who permitted him to love them. He had many adventures in arms and in gallantry, and great misadventures. Later he was killed by a foot-soldier.

[1] Catalonia. Northeastern region of Spain.
[2] Medieval *condado* (county) in the northern portion of Catalonia, in the province of Barcelona.
[3] The castle of Madrona (or Castell Berguedà), near Berga, in Barcelona.
[4] Puig-reig (*Riechs* is a corrupted form).
[5] Raimon was, in fact, assassinated in 1175. See M. Riquer, *Guillem de Berguedà* I, 28-32, for discussion of the vida, and *passim* for texts of the 32 extant poems. Cardona is in Catalonia, south of Berga.
[6] Viscount Arnau de Castellbó, who ruled from 1184 to 1226. Castellbó is in the diocese of Urgel, in Catalonia.

52. GUILLEM DE CABESTAING (CABESTAN, CABESTANH)

A. Version of manuscripts *FbIK*

Guillem de Cabestaing[1] was a knight from the region of Roussillon,[2] which borders on Catalonia and Narbonnais.[3] He was a very charming man, distinguished in arms and in gallantry and in courtliness. And there was in his region a lady called Lady Soremonda,[4] wife of Lord Raimon de Castel Rossillon,[5] who was very rich and noble, and wicked and fierce and cruel and haughty. And Guillem de Cabestaing truly loved the lady and sang about her and composed his songs about her.[6] And the lady, who was young and noble and beautiful and charming, loved him more than anything in the world.

And this was told to Lord Raimon de Castel Roussillon. And he, like an angry and jealous man, investigated the matter, and learned that it was true. And he ordered that his wife be carefully watched. And it so happened that one day Raimon de Castel Roussillon came upon Guillem passing by without great company, and he killed him. And he took the heart out of his body, and had it taken to a squire in his house, and had it cooked and peppered, and gave it to his wife to eat.

And when the lady had eaten the heart of Lord Guillem de Cabestaing, Lord Raimon told her what it was. And when she heard it, she lost her sense of sight and her hearing. And when she came to, she said, "Lord, you have given me such a good thing to eat, that I shall never eat again." And when he heard what she said, he ran with his sword intending to strike her on the head. But she ran to the balcony and threw herself down; and she was killed.[7]

---

[1] Cabestaing is today Capestany, in the arrondissement of Perpignan (Pyrénées-Orientales).

[2] Ancient county in southern Languedoc.

[3] Region around Narbonne (Aude).

[4] Saurimonda of Peiralda. Peiralda is a castle near Torreilles, in the canton of Rivesaltes, arrondissement of Perpignan (Pyrénées-Orientales).

[5] Raimon de Castel-Roussillon (east of Perpignan in the Pyrénées-Orientales) married Saurimonda in 1197.

[6] Two out of Guillem's seven songs (and one of dubious attribution) are addressed to "En Raimon"; see A. Langfors, *Les chansons de Guillem de Cabestaing*, (Paris, 1924), Nos. 3.52, 5.96, 9.57; the vidas are discussed, pp. vii-xviii.

[7] Ezra Pound compares this vida with the Greek myth of the eating of Itys' body in the Tereus-Procne-Philomela legend; see Canto 4, pp. 13-16. It was also told by Boccaccio in his *Decameron*, Fourth Day, Ninth Tale with Cabestaing called Guardastagno.

B. Version of manuscripts *ABN²*

Guillem de Cabestaing was a knight from the region of Roussillon, which borders on Catalonia and Narbonnais. He was a very handsome man in appearance, and very distinguished in arms and courtliness and gallantry. And there was in his region a lady called Lady Soremonda, wife of Lord Raimon de Castel Rossillon, who was very noble and rich and wicked and fierce and cruel and haughty. Lord Guillem de Cabestaing truly loved the lady and sang about her and composed his songs about her. And the lady, who was young and gay and noble and beautiful, loved him more than anything in the world.

And this was told to Lord Raimon de Castel Roussillon. And he, like an angry and jealous man, investigated all the facts and learned that they were true. And he ordered that his wife be watched. And one day Raimon de Castel Roussillon came upon Guillem de Cabestaing, who was passing by without great company, and he killed him. And he had the heart taken out of the body, and had the head cut off. And he had the heart carried to his house, and the head too. And he had the heart cooked and peppered, and had it given to his wife to eat.

And when the lady had eaten it, Raimon de Castel Roussillon said to her, "Do you know what you have eaten?"

And she said to him, "No, except that it was a good and delicious meat."

And he told her that it was the heart of Lord Guillem de Cabestaing that she had eaten. And, so that she would really believe him, he had the head brought in before her. And when the lady saw and heard this, she lost her sense of sight and her hearing. And when she came to, she said, "Lord, you have given me such a good thing to eat that I shall never eat again."

And when he heard this, he ran with his sword, intending to strike her on the head. And she ran to a balcony and threw herself down, and in this way she died.

And the news circulated around Roussillon and throughout Catalonia that Lord Guillem de Cabestaing and the lady had died in such a bad way, and that Lord Raimon de Castel Roussillon had given Lord Guillem's heart to the lady to eat. There was great sadness in all the regions, and a complaint was addressed to the King of Aragon,[1] who was the overlord of Lord Raimon de Castel Roussillon and of Lord Guillem de Cabestaing. And he came to Perpignan, in Roussillon, and made Raimon de Castel Roussillon come before him. And when he had come, he had him apprehended and took all his castles away from him, and had them destroyed. And he took away everything he had and put him in prison.

And later he had the bodies of Guillem de Cabestaing and the lady taken and carried to Perpignan and placed in a tomb in front of the door of the church. And he had the way in which they had died depicted on the tomb. And he ordered that all the knights and the ladies of the entire county of Roussillon should come yearly to celebrate the anniversary of their death. And Raimon de Castel Roussillon died in the king's prison.

---

[1] Alfonso of Aragon had died in 1196, a year before the marriage of Saurimonda and Raimon. Langfors points out that the author of this version tries to render the text more authentic by referring to specific historical events (*Chansons de G. de Cabestaing*, p. xv.)

53.   GUILLEM FIGUEIRA

Guillem Figuera[1] was from Toulouse, the son of a tailor,
and he was a tailor also.   And when the French took
Toulouse,[2] he came to Lombardy.   And he knew how to invent
poetry well and how to sing.   And he became a minstrel among
the citizens.   He was not a man who would know how to fit
among the barons or among high society.   But he was greatly
cherished by rogues and harlots and innkeepers and
publicans.   And if he saw a notable man from the court come
where he was, he became sad and afflicted.   And at once he
would take pains to debase him and to exalt the rabble.

---

[1] More commonly Figueira.   Texts of his ten poems are to
   be found in E. Levy, *Guilhem Figueira, ein
   provenzalischer Troubadour* (Berlin, 1880).
[2] In 1229, at the end of the Albigensian Crusade, when
   Raimon VII opened the doors of Toulouse to the
   "French" before negotiating with Louis IX and the
   papal legate in Paris.

54.   GUILLEM MAGRET

Guillem Magret was a minstrel from Viennois,[1] a gambler
and a publican.   And he composed good songs and good
sirventes and good couplets.[2]   And he was well liked and
honored, but he never rode well-equipped because everything
that he earned he gambled and spent in an evil fashion at
the tavern.   Later he entered a hospital in Spain,[3] in the
land of Lord Roiz Peire dels Gambiaros.[4]

---

[1] Region of Vienne (Isère).
[2] See F. Naudieth, *Der Trobador Guilhem Magret* (Halle,
   1914) for Guillem's eight poems.
[3] Guillem's poems indicate that he frequented the courts
   of Pedro II of Aragon (1196-1213) and of Alfonso IX

(1187-1230). The hospital he entered is unknown.
[4] Pedro Ruíz de los Cameros was related to Rodrigo Díaz
de los Cameros, a Castilian lord who commanded an army
in the battle of Las Navas.

55. GUILLEM DE MONTANHAGOL (MONTAIGNAGOL)

Guillem de Montanhagol[1] was a knight from Provence, and was
a good inventor of poetry, and a great lover. And he was in
love with Lady Jauseranda,[2] from the castle of Lunel.[3] And
he composed many good songs for her.

[1] Montanhagol means "from Montanhac." It is not known
which town of Montanhac was Guillem's home. For a
discussion of this poet's origin and identity, and an
edition of his fourteen poems, see P. Ricketts, *Les
Poésies de Guillem de Montanhagol, troubadour
provençal du XIIIe siècle* (Toronto, 1964).
[2] Unknown lady mentioned in P.-C. 225.1, line 11. See
J. Coulet, *Le Troubadour Guillem de Montaignagol*
(Toulouse, 1898), pp. 24-25.
[3] Lunel is the seat of a canton in Hérault. It seems
that Guillem knew Raymond Gaucelm V, the lord of
Lunel.

57. GUILLEM RAINOL D'AT

Guillem Rainol d'At was a knight from the city of Apt,[1]
which is in the county of Forcalquier.[2] He was a good
inventor of *sirventes*[3] about the rumors which circulated in
Provence concerning the King of Aragon[4] and the Count of

Toulouse.[5] And he composed new melodies for all his
sirventes. He was greatly feared by all the barons because
of the caustic *sirventes* he composed.

[1] Seat of a canton in the arrondissement of Cavaillon
    (Vaucluse).
[2] Seat of an arrondissement in the Basses-Alpes. This
    county occupied most of the Haute-Provence between the
    Alps and the regions of Isère and Durance.
[3] No edition exists of his five poems; see Riquer, *Los
    Trovadores*, III, 1236-1246, for texts, translations
    and notes on three poems.
[4] Perhaps Pedro II, killed at Muret in 1216 (?).
[5] Either Raimon VI or Raimon VII of Toulouse.

57. GUILLEM DE SAINT LEIDIER

Guillem de Saint Leidier[1] was a rich castellan from
Velay,[2] from the bishopric of the Puoi Sainta Maria.[3] And
he was an honored man, a capable knight and generous giver
of his wealth, who was very learned and very courtly, and
was a very true lover who was very much loved and esteemed.
And he courted Marquesa of Polonhac,[4] who was the sister of
Dalfin d'Alvernhe[5] and Lady Sail de Claustra,[6] and the
wife of the Viscount of Polonhac. Lord Guilhem de Saint
Leidier composed his songs about her and truly loved her and
called her "Bertran."[7] And he also called Lord Ugo
Marescal[8] "Bertran." He was his companion and knew
everything that Guilhem de Saint Leidier and the marquess
did and said. And the three of them called one another
"Bertran." The three of them experienced great happiness
together, it turned to sadness for Lord Guilhem de Saint
Leidier, because the other two Bertrans wronged him greatly.

[1] Also Saint-Didier. Saint-Didier-la-Séauve (in Yssin-
    geaux, Haute-Loire) is today Saint-Didier-en-Velay.

² Seat of Le Puy (Haute-Loire).
³ Le Puy. Ancient *Podium Aniciense*, where the Virgin of
   Mont Anis was venerated.
⁴ Daughter of Count Guilhem VII of Auvergne, wife of
   Eracle III, Viscount of Polignac (died 1198).
   Marquesa, according to Boutière-Schutz (p. 273), is
   here a proper name, attributed to her by analogy with
   her grandmother. Polonhac is today Polignac, in the
   arrondissement and canton of Puy, Haute-Loire.
⁵ Dauphin of Auvergne. See Vida 101, note 8, and Vida
   27.
⁶ Sail de Claustra (meaning "escaped from the cloister")
   was the wife of Béraut III of Mercoeur. She is
   mentioned also in Vida 79.
⁷ *Senhal* which appears in many of Guilhem's thirteen
   songs. See A. Sakari, *Poésies du troubadour Guillem
   de Saint-Didier* (Helsinki, 1956), texts Nos. 2, 3, 4,
   5, 6, 7, 12, 13.
⁸ Unknown person.

58. GUILLEM DE LA TOR

Guillem de la Tor was a minstrel,[1] who was from
Perigord, from a castle called La Tor.[2] And he went to
Lombardy. And he knew many songs, and created and sang well
and graciously, and he also invented. But when he wanted to
recite his songs, he made his discussion of the explanation
longer than the song itself. And he took a wife in Milan,
who was beautiful and young, the wife of a barber, whom he
abducted and took away to Como.[3] And he loved her more than
anything in the world.

And it came to pass that she died. He was so afflicted
by this that he became mad and believed that she was
pretending to be dead in order to leave him. So he left her
ten days and ten nights on the tomb [...][4] And every
evening he would go to the tomb and carry her outside and
look at her face, kissing and embracing her and asking her

59

to speak to him and tell him whether she was dead or alive; and if she were alive, that she return to him, and if she were dead, that she tell him what afflictions she was suffering; that he would have so many masses given for her and he would give so many alms that he would free her from those afflictions.

This became known in the city by the notable men, so that the people of the place had him go away from there. And he looked everywhere for sorcerers and sorceresses [to tell him] if she could ever be brought back to life. And a trickster led him to believe that if he read the Psalter every day and recited 150 *Pater nosters* and gave alms to seven poor persons before he ate, and if he did this for a whole year, without missing a day, she would come back to life, but would not eat or drink or talk. And he was very pleased when he heard this, and began at once to do what this trickster had directed him to do. And so he did this for an entire year without missing a single day. And when he saw that what he had been taught was of no avail, he despaired and allowed himself to die.

[1] For his 14 poems, see F. Blasi, *Le Poesie de Guillem de la Tor* (Geneva/Florence, 1934).
[2] La Tor is generally thought to be near what is today Tour-Blanche, not far from Verteillac, arrondissement of Ribérac (Dordogne).
[3] City in Lombardy.
[4] This passage presents textual difficulties. There seems to be a *lacuna* between "el la laisset dez dias e dez nuoigz sobre.l monimen" and the following sentence which varies in manuscripts *I* and *K*. *I* gives: "chascun ser lauaua el monimen"; *K* "chascun ser el leuaua (or "lanaua") lo monumen". Boutière-Schutz (pp. 236-237) suggest the following corrections: "el anava [a]l monumen" (he went to the tomb) or "el levava la monumen" (he picked up the tombstone). Favati proposes the latter reading (p. 324).

59. GUIRAUDO LO ROS

Guiraudo lo Ros[1] was from Toulouse, the son of a poor knight. And he came to the court of his lord, the Count Anfos,[2] to serve him. And he was courtly and a good singer. And he fell in love with the countess, daughter of his lord, and his love for her taught him how to invent poetry. And he composed many songs.

[1] Guiraudet le Roux ("the redhead" or "the blond"). For an edition of Guiraudo's eight poems see A. M. Finoli, "Le poesie di Guiraudo lo Ros", *Studi Medievali*, *15* (1974), 1-57; also Riquer, *Los Trovadores*, II, 670-674.

[2] Probably the younger brother of Raimon V of Toulouse and son of Alfonse Jourdain. He died in 1185. It is not known if he did in fact have any daughters.

60. JAUFRE RUDEL

A. Version of manuscripts *AB*

Jaufre Rudel de Blaia was a very noble man, the prince of Blaye.[1] And he fell in love with the Countess of Tripoli[2] without seeing her, because of the great good and the great nobility he had heard tell of her by pilgrims returning from Antioch.[3] And he composed many good poems about her with good melodies and poor words (rhymes?).[4] Determined to see her, he took the cross and sailed away to see her. And then he was taken so gravely ill on board that those with him thought he would die. But they did at least take him to Tripoli to a shelter, thinking him dead. And it was made known to the countess, and she came to him, to his bedside, and took him in her arms. And he knew that she was the countess, so he recovered his sight and his sense of smell, and praised God and thanked Him for having sustained his life until he had seen her. And thus he died in the arms of the countess. And she had him buried with honor in the House of the Temple[5] in Tripoli. And afterwards, on that same day, she became a nun because of the grief she felt about him and about his death. And here are written some of his songs.

[1] Seat of an arrondissement in Gironde.
[2] A county founded in Syria by the counts of Toulouse during the Crusades.
[3] City located in what is now southern Turkey.
[4] Problematic phrase. Boutière-Schutz translate, "avec de bonnes mélodies [mais] de pauvres mots " (p. 18); Riquer gives "con buen son y pobres palabras" (*Los Trovadores*, I, 154); Bertolucci Pizzorusso translates, "e fece su di lei molte canzoni, di cui le melodie erano piu pregevoli dei versi," ("Il grado zero," pp. 7-26).
[5] Institution of the Knight Templars. The story of this vida forms the basis for Edmond Rostand's early play, *La Princesse Lointaine* (1895).

B. Version of manuscripts *IK*

Jaufre Rudel de Blaia was a very noble man, prince of Blaye, and he fell in love with the Countess of Tripoli without seeing her, because of the good which he had heard tell of her by the pilgrims who returned from Antioch. And he composed many poems about her with good melodies but with poor words. And resolved to see her, he took the cross and sailed; and he was taken ill on board ship and was taken to Tripoli, to an inn, as if he were dead.

And it was made known to the countess, and she came to him, to his bedside, and took him in her arms. And he knew that she was the countess, and he immediately recovered his sight and his sense of smell and praised God who had sustained his life until he had seen her. And thus he died in her arms. And she had him buried with great honor in the

house of the Temple and on that same day she became a nun
because of the grief she had experienced at his death.

61. JORDAN BONEL

Jordan Bonel was from Saintonge,[1] from the march of
Poitou. And he composed many good songs about Lady Gitbors
de Montausier,[2] who was the wife of the Count of
Angoulême[3] and later was the wife of the Lord of
Mon[t]auzier[4] and of Barbezieux[5] and of Chalais.[6]

[1] Region in western France (Charente-Maritime).
[2] Guibourc de Montausier is also mentioned in Bertran de
Born's *razo* of 80.38. Historical inaccuracies in this
vida and in the *razo* are discussed in Boutière-Schutz,
pp. 84-85, note 1. No edition has yet been published
of the three extant poems of Jordan Bonel.
[3] Today seat of the department of Charente-Maritime,
Angoulême was the ancient capital of the Angoumois.
[4] City in the arrondissement of Cognac (Charente).
[5] Seat of a canton in the arrondissement of Cognac
(Charente).
[6] Seat of a canton in the arrondissement of Angoulême
(Charente).

62. LANFRANC CIGALA

Lord Lanfranc Cigala was from the city of Genoa. He was
a noble and learned man. And he was a judge and a knight,
but he led the life of a judge. And he was a great lover;
and he was interested in inventing poetry and was a good
inventor, and he composed many good songs.[1] And he often
invented poetry about God. And here are written some of his
songs.

[1] See F. Branciforti, *Il Canzoniere di Lanfranco Cigala*,
(Florence, 1954), for the texts of the 32 poems.

63. LOMBARDA, NA

(Razo of P.-C. 54.1 and P.-C. 288.1)

Lady Lombarda was a lady from Toulouse, noble and
beautiful and charming in appearance and learned. And she
knew how to invent well, and she composed beautiful couplets
about love.[1] So Bernart Lord Arnaut,[2] brother of the count
of Armagnac, heard tell of her goodness and her merit. And
he came to Toulouse to see her. And he was with her in
great privacy and asked for her love and was very much her
friend. And he composed these couplets about her, and sent
them to her, to her house. And afterwards he mounted his
horse without seeing her and went away to his land:

I would like to be a Lombard for Lady Lombarda
For neither Alamanda nor Giscarda please me
                                    as much
With her pleasing eyes she looks at me in
                                    such a way
That she seems to be offering me her love;
                        but how long it takes.
        For she has beauty
        And my pleasure

And her smile under such close guard
That no one can remove them.

Lord Jourdan, if I leave you Germany
France and Poitiers, Normandy and Brittany,
You must leave me without dispute
Lombardy, Livorno, and Lomagna
      And if you help me,
      I will tenfold
      Increase your wealth with her to whom
      All evil is foreign.

      Mirror-of-Merit
      You give me solace.
      Let the love you have for me
      Never be broken for a plebeian.[3]

Lady Lombarda greatly marvelled when she heard that Bernart
Lord Arnaut had gone away without seeing her, and she sent
him these couplets:

I would like to be called Lady Bernarda for
                             Bernart,
And Lady Arnauda for Lord Arnaut.
Many thanks, lord, for it pleases you
To have named me with two such ladies.
      I want you to tell me
      Which one pleases you most
      --Without secrets--
      And which is the mirror where you
                    stare.

For to have a mirror and not look into it is so
Disturbing to my peace that it almost
                  shatters it.
But when I remember what my name recalls,
All my thoughts are resolved harmoniously.
      But I wonder where
      You have put your heart.
      I can neither see its house nor its
                 cottage,
      For you have hidden them.[4]

[1] See Schultz-Gora, pp. 10 and 22; Bogin, pp. 114-117.
[2] Bernart Arnaut, brother and successor of Geraud IV.
   He was Count of Armagnac from 1217-1226.
[3] [L]ombards volgr'eu eser per Na Lombarda
   Q'Alamanda no.m plaz tan ni Giscarda;
   Qar ab sos oiltz plaisenz tan jen mi garda
   Qe par qe.m don s'amor; mas trop me tarda
         Qar bel veser
         E mon plaiser
      Ten e bel ris en garda,
      C'om no.ls ne pod mover.

Segner Jordan, se vos lais Alamagna,
Fransa e Piteus, Normandia e Bertagna,
Be me devez laisar senes mesclagna
Lombardia, Livorno e Lomagna;
         E si.m valez,
         Eu per un dez
      Valdre.us ab leis, q'estragna
      De s[e] tot avol prez.

         [M]irail-de-Pres,
         Conort avez;
      Ges per vila no.s fragna
      L'amor en qe.m tenez. (P.-C. 54.1)
[4] [N]om volgr'aver per Bernard Na Bernarda
   E per N'Arnaut N'Arnauda [estre] apellada;
   E gran[s] merses, seigner, car vos agrada
   C'ab tal[s] doas domnas m'aves nomnada;
         Voil qe.m digaz
         Cal mais vos plaz,
         Ses cuberta selada,
         E.l mirail on miraz.

Car lo marailz e no ueser descorda
Tan mon acord c'ab pauc no.l desacorda;
Mes can record so qe.l meus noms recorda,
En bon acord totz mons pensars s'acorda;
         Mas del cor pes
         On l'aves mes,
         Qe sa maiso ni borda
         No vei, qe las taises. (P.-C. 288.1)

64. MARCABRU (MARCABRUN)

A. Version of manuscript *K*

Marcabru was from Gascony,[1] the son of a poor woman who was named Marcabruna, as he says himself in his song:

Marcabru, son of lady Bruna,
Was begotten beneath such a moon
That he knew how love sheds its seed
    -Listen!-
For he has never loved a woman
Nor been loved by any.[2]

He was one of the first inventors of poetry whom people remember. He composed bad poems and bad *sirventes*, and he maligned women and love.

[1] The only biographical information we possess about Marcabru comes from these vidas; his Gáscon origin seems to be supported by linguistic peculiarities in the poems.

[2] Marcabruns, lo fills Na Bruna,
Fo engendraz en tal luna
Qu'el saup d'amor cum degruna,
    -Escoutatz!-
Que anc non amet neguna,
Ni d'autra no fo amatz. (P.-C. 293.18)
For a critical edition of Marcabru's 44 poems, see J. M. L. Dejeanne, *Poésies complètes du troubadour Marcabru* (Toulouse, 1909).

B. Version of manuscript *A*

Marcabru was abandoned at the door of a rich man and no one ever knew who he was nor from where he came. And Lord Aldric del Vilar[1] brought him up. Afterwards he lived so long with an inventor of poetry called Cercamon[2] that he himself began to invent poems. Previously he had been called Panperdut,[3] but from then on he was called Marcabru.

And at that time songs were not called *cansos*, rather everything that was sung was called *vers*. And Marcabru enjoyed great renown and was heard throughout the world. And he was feared on account of his tongue, for he was so given to calumny that finally the lords of the manor of Guyenne, of whom he had spoken great ill, had him undone.

[1] Aldric d'Auvillars' poem addressed to Marcabru is extant (P.-C. 166.1). Auvillars is in the department of Tarn et Garonne.

[2] See Vida 24. This information is suspect; none of Cercamon's datable poems predates the works of Marcabru.

[3] Professional pseudonym composed of *pan*, "bread," and *perdut*, "lost." Cf. R. Lejeune, "Le chien Pan-perdu".

65. MARIA DE VENTADORN

(Razo of P.-C. 295.1)

You have surely heard of my lady Maria de Ventadorn,[1] how she was the most esteemed lady who ever lived in Limousin, and the one who did the most good and who most kept herself from evil. And her reason always helped her, and folly never made her act foolishly. And God honored her with a beautifully pleasing body, without any artifice. Lord Gui d'Uisel[2] had lost his lady, as you have heard in his song which says:

If you part me, evil lady, from you[3]

so he lived in great pain and in great sadness. And he had not sung or invented poetry in a long time, and all the good ladies from that region were very grieved about it, and Lady Maria more than any other, for Lord Gui d'Uisel praised her in all his songs. And the Count of La Marche,[4] who was

called Lord Uc lo Brun,[5] was her knight, and she had
granted him as much honor and as much love as a lady can
bestow on a knight. And one day as he was courting her,
they had an argument between them: the Count of La Marche
said that every true lover, from the time his lady gives him
her love and takes him as her knight and friend, must have,
in as much as he is loyal and true to her, as much
suzerainty and authority from her as she has from him. And
Lady Maria forbade that the friend should have suzerainty or
authority over her. Lord Gui d'Uisel was in the court of
Lady Maria and she, to make him return to his songs and his
joy, composed a couplet in which she asked him if it was
proper for the friend to have as much suzerainty over the
lady as she had over him. And on this subject my lady Maria
challenged him to a *tenson* exchange, and said thus:

Gui d'Ussel, you grieve me greatly.[6]

---

[1] Maria was the daughter of Raimon II of Turenne. She
married Ebles V, Viscount of Ventadour, and died
around 1222. Her poems appear in J. Audiau, *Les
Poésies des quatre troubadours d'Ussel* (Paris, 1922)
pp. 73 ff.; Schultz-Gora, pp. 21 ff.; Bogin, pp.
98-101.
[2] See Vida 45.
[3] Si be.m partetz, mala dompna, de vos (P.-C. 194.19).
[4] Northwestern area of the Massif Central, between
Limousin and Combrailles.
[5] Hugues IX, Count of La Marche, who died in 1219.
[6] Gui d'Uisel, be.m pesa de vos (P.-C. 295.1).

66. LO MONGES DE MONTAUDON (THE MONK OF MONTAUDON)

The Monk of Montaudon[1] was from Auvergne, from a castle
named Vic,[2] which is near Aurillac.[3] He was a noble man,
and he was made a monk of the abbey of Aurillac.[4] And the

abbot gave him the priorate of Montaudon, and there he endeavored to do much for the good of the house. And he composed couplets while he was in the monastery and *sirventes* on subjects that were popular in that region.[5]

And the knights and the barons took him away from the monastery and honored him greatly and gave him whatever he wished for or requested. And he took everything back to Montaudon, to his priorate. He greatly increased and improved his church, while still wearing the monk's habit. And he returned to Aurillac, to his abbot, showing him the improvements he had made on the priorate of Montaudon. And he begged him to grant him the privilege of following the desire of the king, Lord Anfos d'Aragon.[6] And the abbot gave it to him.

And the king ordered him to eat meat and court women and sing and invent poetry. And he did so. And he was made lord of the Puy Sainta Maria and was chosen for the giving of the sparrow-hawk.[7] For a long time he had the suzerainty of the court of Puy until the court was dissolved.

And afterwards he went to Spain and was greatly honored by all the kings and all the barons. And he went to a priorate in Spain named Villafranca[8] which belongs to the abbey of Aurillac. And the abbot gave it to him. And he enriched it and improved it. And there he died and ended his days.

---

[1] The town of Montaudon has not been identified; sometimes believed to be Montauban or another place.
[2] Vic-sur-Cère. The seat of a canton in the arrondissement of Aurillac (Cantal).
[3] Chief town of the department of Cantal (Basse-Auvergne).
[4] It belonged to the diocese of Clermont until 1316.
[5] See O. Klein, *Die Dichtungen des Mönchs von Montaudon* (Marburg, 1885).
[6] One of Alfonso II of Aragon's vassals was the viscount of Carlat, lord of Vic.
[7] The court of Puy (*Podium Aniciense*) was a poetical society which granted a sparrow-hawk as a prize. In manuscript *A*, folio 120, the Monk is shown holding the sparrow-hawk.
[8] Probably the Benedictine priorate of Saint-Pierre-

de-Belloc, near Villefranche-de-Conflent, in Prades (Pyrénées-Orientales) Roussillon. Contrary to what the vida says, this monastery did not depend on Aurillac (Boutière-Schutz, p. 310).

67. PEIRE D'ALVERNHE

Peire d'Alvernhe was from the bishopric of Clermont.[1] He was a wise man and well versed in letters, and was the son of a burgher. He was handsome and charming in person, he invented well and sang well, and he was the first good inventor of poetry to go beyond the mountains, and the one who wrote the best melodies for poems ever composed:

At the time of brief days and long evenings.[2]

He did not compose any *cansos*, for songs were not called *cansos* then, but *vers*, since Lord Giraut de Borneill[3] composed the first song that was ever made. Peire was very honored and esteemed by all the worthy barons of the time and by all the worthy ladies. And he was considered the best inventor of poetry in the world until Giraut de Borneill appeared. He praised himself greatly in his songs and blamed the other inventors, so that he says [this] about himself in a couplet of one of his *sirventes*:

Peire d'Alverne has such a voice
That he sings high and low
And his melodies are sweet and pleasant
And, still, he is master of all.
If only he would make his words clear
Since one can hardly understand them.[4]

He stayed and lived in this world for a long time with the high society according to what Dalfin d'Alvernhe,[5] who was born during his time, tells me. And afterwards, he did penance and died.

71

[1] Clermont-Ferrand, seat of the department of Puy-de-Dôme.

[2] De josta.ls breus jorns e.ls loncs sers (P.-C. 323.15).
For the 24 poems of Peire d'Alvernhe, see A. del Monte, *Peire d'Alvernha, Liriche* (Turin, 1955).

[3] See Vida 41.

[4] Peire d'Alverne a tal votz
Que canta de sobr'e de sotz
E siei son son douz e plasen
E pos es maistre de totz
Ab q'un pauc esclaris sos motz
Qu'a penas nuillz hom los enten (P.-C. 323.11).

[5] Dauphin of Auvergne, (Vida 27) also knew Uc de Saint Circ. This reference to Dalfin suggests to some that Uc might be the author of the vida. Dalfin is not a title, but a proper name attested in Auvergne before 1100; see S. C. Aston, "The Name".

68. PEIRE DE BARJAC

Peire de Barjac[1] was a knight, companion of Guillem de Balaun.[2] And he was very able and courtly, and precisely such a knight as was fitting for Guillem de Balaun. And he also fell in love with a lady from the castle of Jaujac,[3] the wife of a minor noble, and she with him. And he received from her everything he pleased. And Guillem de Balaun knew of the love between them. And it so happened that one evening he came to Jaujac with Guillem de Balaun, and he sat down to converse with his lady. And it so happened that Peire de Barjac left her in a bad way, and with great displeasure because of the disdainful leave she had given him. And when the following day came, Guillem left, and Peire went with him sad and grieving. Lord Guillem asked him why he was so sad, and he told him the reason. Lord Guillem comforted him by telling him that he would reconcile them. And it was not long before they returned to Jaujac and they were reconciled. And Peire left her, [delighted] with the great pleasure she had given him. And here is written the farewell he gave her.

[1] Barjac is a commune in the arrondissement of Alès (Gard).
[2] See Vida 50.
[3] Jaujac (old *Gaudacium*) now a commune in the canton of Thueyts, arrondissement of Largentière (Ardèche).

69. PEIRE BREMON LO TORT

Peire Bremon lo Tort was a poor knight from Viennois,[1] and he was a good inventor of poetry and was honored by all the notable men.

[1] Region around Vienne (Isère). For an edition of Peire's poems, see J. Boutière, "Peire Bremon Lo Tort", *Romania*, *54* (1928), 427-452.

70. PEIRE DE BUSSIGNAC

Peire de Bussignac[1] was a cleric, a nobleman from Hautefort,[2] from the castle of Lord Bertran de Born. He invented good *sirventes* to reproach the ladies who behaved badly and to attack the *sirventes* of Bertran de Born.

[1] Either Boussignac (canton of Tulle, Corrèze) or Bussignac (canton of Hautefort, Dordogne). According to Boutière-Schutz, the latter is more likely (p. 145).
[2] In the arrondissement of Périgueux (Dordogne); see Vida 17.

71. PEIRE CARDENAL

Peire Cardenal was from Velay,[1] from the city of Puy Nostra Domna.[2] And he was from an honorable family of rank, the son of a knight and of a lady. And when he was little, his father had him enter the highest canonry of Puy as a canon. And he learned his letters and knew well how to read and sing. And when he reached the age of manhood, he found pleasure in the vanity of this world, for he was gay and handsome and young. And he invented poetry about many beautiful subjects with beautiful tunes.[3]

And he composed songs, but few of them. And he composed many *sirventes*, and his invention was very beautiful and good. In these *sirventes* he showed many good subjects and good examples, if they are well understood. For he condemned very strongly the folly of this world and greatly reproached false clerics, as his *sirventes* show. And he went around the courts of kings and noble barons, taking with him his minstrel, who sang his *sirventes*. And he was very honored and esteemed by my lord the good king Jaime of Aragon[4] and by honorable barons.

And I, Master Miquel de la Tor,[5] writer, make it known that Lord Peire Cardenal, when he passed from this life, was very close to one hundred years old. And I, the aforesaid Miquel, have written these *sirventes* in the city of Nîmes.[6] And here are written some of his *sirventes*.

---

[1] Seat of Le Puy. His last name is sometimes spelled Cardinal.

[2] Puy Notre-Dame or Le Puy-en-Velay.

[3] See R. Lavaud, *Poésies complètes du troubadour Peire Cardenal (1180-1278)* (Toulouse, 1957), for texts of the 96 poems.

[4] Jaime I of Aragon, called "The Conqueror" (1213-1276).

[5] Miquel de la Tor also compiled a collection--now lost--of troubadour poems, *Lo Libro de Michele*. This is one of the rare cases in which a vida author identifies himself; see also Vida 14 where Uc de Saint Circ, the other known vida composer, does the same.

[6] Seat of the department of Gard.

72. PEIRE GUILLEM OF TOULOUSE

Peire Guillem was from Toulouse, a courtly man and one
who was delighted to be among high society. And he composed
couplets well, but he composed too many of them. And he
composed *sirventes* in the manner of jongleurs[1] and [others]
to criticize the barons. And he entered the order of
Spaza.[2]

[1] The text gives *sirventes joglarescs*. See S. Mejean,
"Contribution", for a definition of this genre, which
is also mentioned in Vidas 34 and 49.
[2] Order of the Sword (?).

73. PEIRE DE MAENSAC

Peire de Maensac[1] was from Auvergne, from the land of
the Dalfin,[2] and he was a poor knight. And he had a
brother named Austors de Maensac,[3] and both of them were
inventors of poetry. And they were both in agreement that
one of them would have the castle, and the other would be an
inventor. Austor had the castle, and Peire was the
inventor, and he invented poems about the wife of Lord
Bernart de Tierci.[4] He sang about her so much and honored
her and served her so much that the lady allowed herself to
be abducted by him.

inventor, and he invented poems about the wife of Lord
Bernart de Tierci.[4] He sang about her so much and honored
her and served her so much that the lady allowed herself to
be abducted by him.

And he took her to a castle of the Dalfin d'Alvernhe.
The husband forcefully claimed her, with the help of the
Church, by waging a great war. And the Dalfin defended the
husband so well that he never gave her back. He was an
extremely able man and a pleasant companion. And he
composed songs with pleasing melodies and words, and good
tensos.[5]

[1] Maensac is either Mauzat, in the arrondissement of
Riom (Puy-de-Dôme), or Mainsat, in the arrondissement
of Aubusson (Creuse). See Ezra Pound's Canto 5.
[2] See Vida 27.
[3] According to Chabaneau (*Biographies des Troubadours*,
p. 265, note 2) the troubadour is often confused with
Astorgins de Mayencac, *domicellus*, mentioned in a
document of 1238. There are no extant lyrics of the
troubadour Austor de Maensac.
[4] For discussion of the possible identity of this
unknown person, see Boutière-Schutz, p. 302.
[5] The text gives *coblas de solatz*. Boutière-Schutz
render it "de bons couplets divertissants" (p. 302),
but with Bergin, I prefer *tenso* (*Anthology*, II, p.
228).

74. PEIRE DE LA MULA

Peire de la Mula was a minstrel who stayed in
Montferrat[1] in Piemonte with Lord Ot del Carretto,[2] and
also in Cortemiglia.[3] And he was an inventor of couplets
and of *sirventes*.

[1] The Marquisate of Montferrat, in Italy, included much

75. PEIRE RAIMON OF TOULOUSE

Peire Raimon of Toulouse lo Viellz[1] was the son of a burgher. And he became a minstrel and went to the court of King Alfonso of Aragon.[2] And the king welcomed him and bestowed great honor upon him. And he was a wise and clever man, and he knew well how to invent poetry and how to sing. And he composed good songs. And he was in the court of the king and of the good Count Raimon[3] and of the Lord Guillem de Montpellier[4] for a long time. Later he took a wife in Pamiers.[5] And there he ended his days. And here are written some of his songs.

[1] It is uncertain whether *lo Viellz* (which only appears in manuscripts *ABN²*) means "the elder" or indicates that Peire belonged to an older generation; see Boutière-Schutz, p. 348, note 1. For his poetry (18 texts), see A. Cavalière, *Le Poesie di Peire Raimon de Tolosa* (Florence, 1935).

[2] Alfonso II (1162-1196).

[3] Either Raimon V (1148-1194) or, more plausibly, Raimon VI (1194-1222).

[4] Probably Guillaume VIII (died 1202), who received several troubadours at his court, including Giraut de Calanso, Aimeric de Sarlat, and Arnaut de Marueil, and is mentioned as a patron of poets in Raimon Vidal's *Abrils issia*.

[5] Town in Ariège.

76. PEIRE ROGIER

Peire Rogier was from Auvergne and was a canon of
Clermont.[1] And he was a noble man, handsome and charming,
well versed in letters and with a natural wit, and he sang
and invented poems well.

And he left the canonry and became a minstrel and went
around the courts, and his songs were praised. And he went
to Narbonne,[2] to the court of Lady Ermengarda,[3] who was
then of great worth and of great merit. And she greeted him
well and gave him great favors. And he fell in love with
her and composed his poems and his songs about her. And she
welcomed them. And he called her "Tort-n'avez."[4]

He was at her court for a long time, and it was believed
that he received the pleasures of love from her. She was
blamed for this by the people of that region. And for fear
of what people might say, she gave him permission to go and
had him leave her. And he went sad and thoughtful and
troubled and downcast to Lord Raimbaut d'Aurenga,[5] as he
says in the *sirventes* he composed about him:

Lord Raimbaut, to see your
Encouragement and your company,
I came here early and promptly,
But I am not here for your money
For I wish to know, when I leave,
If the flattery men bestow on you is true
Or if there is more or less
Than I hear said and told about you.

I have so much wit and knowledge
And am so wise and shrewd
That once I have seen your actions
From the beginning, I will know in truth
Whether the praise is as they say,
For they ask me about it there
                    among our people.[6]

He spent a long time with Lord Raimbaut, and was in Spain
with the good King Anfos of Castile[7] and with the good King
Anfos of Aragon[8] and with the good Count Raimon of

78

Toulouse.[9]   He had great honor in the world as long as he
stayed in it, and then he entered the order of Grandmont,[10]
and there he died.

[1] Clermont-Ferrand, in Puy-de-Dôme.
[2] Seat of an arrondissement in the department of Aude.
[3] Viscountess Ermengarde, daughter of Aimeric IV of
    Narbonne (1143-1197), was celebrated by several
    troubadours, among them Bernart de Ventadorn and Peire
    d'Alvernhe.
[4] *Senhal* meaning "You are wrong," which appears in four
    of Peire's songs; see D. T. Nicholson, *The Poems of
    the Troubadour Peire Rogier* (Manchester, 1976), for
    texts of Peire's eight poems.
[5] See Vida 83.
[6] Seign'Raimbautz, per veser
    De vos lo conort e.l solatz
    Son sai vengutz tost e viatz
    Mas que no.n sui per vostr'aver
    Que saber voill, quant m'en partrai
    S'es tals lo gaps com hom lo fai
    E se n'es plus o meinz o mai
    Quom aug dir ni comtar de vos.

    Tant ai de sen e de saber
    E tant sui savis e membratz
    Quant aurai vostres faiz gardatz
    Qu'al partir eu sabrai lo ver
    S'es tals lo gaps com hom retrai
    Qu'enqueron m'en lai entre nos (P.-C. 356.7).
[7] Alfonso VIII (1158-1214).
[8] Alfonso II (1162-1196).
[9] Raimon V (1148-1194).
[10] Grandmont, in the commune of Saint-Sylvestre, canton
    of Laurière (Limoges), is the site of a Benedictine
    abbey.

77. PEIRE DE VALEIRA

Peire de Valeira[1] was from Gascony, from the land of
Lord Arnaut Guillem de Marsan.[2] He was a minstrel at the
very same time in which Marcabru[3] lived, and he composed
poems such as were made at the time, of slight worth, about
leaves and flowers and songs and birds. His songs had no
great value, nor did he.

[1] Also Valera, a place near Podensac and Saint-Macaire
   (Gironde). Peire's two poems have been edited by A.
   Jeanroy: *Jongleurs et troubadours gascons des XIIe et
   XIIIe siècles* (Paris, 1923), pp. 1-3.
[2] A troubadour also mentioned in verse 800 of Raimon
   Vidal's *Abrils issia*, composed around 1200.
[3] See Vida 64. Marcabru lived between 1129-1150.

78. PEIRE VIDAL

Peire Vidal was from Toulouse. He was the son of a
furrier, and he sang better than anyone else in the world.
And he was one of the craziest men who ever were, for he
thought that everything that pleased him or that he wished
for was real. He invented poetry more easily than anyone
else in the world. And he was the one who composed the most
beautiful melodies and who told the greatest follies about
arms and about love and about slander.

And it is true that a knight from Saint Gilles[1] cut his
tongue because Peire pretended that he was his wife's lover.
And Lord Uc des Baux[2] had him cured and treated. And when
he recovered, he went beyond the sea. From there he brought
back a Greek woman who was given to him as a wife in Cyprus.
And he was made to believe that she was the niece of the
Emperor of Constantinople and that by right, thanks to her,
he should have the empire.[3] So he spent all that he could

earn to make a fleet, since he thought of going to conquer the empire. And he bore imperial arms, and he had himself called emperor and his wife empress.

And he also courted all the good ladies he saw and requested the love of them all. And all of them told him to do and to say whatever he wanted. So he thought he was the lover of all of them and that each one of them was dying for him. And all the time he rode fine horses and bore rich arms and [sat on] an imperial throne. He believed himself to be the best knight in the world and the one best loved by the ladies.

[1] Saint-Gilles-du-Gard, in the arrondissment of Nîmes (Gard). For other tales about Peire and an edition of the 45 poems, see D'A. S. Avalle, *Peire Vidal*: *Poésie* (Milan-Naples, 1960); also the poem "Pois Peire d'Alverne a chantat" of the Monk of Montaudon.
[2] Son of Bertran des Baux, Prince of Orange.
[3] This story elaborates metaphors in Peire's lyrics, especially the use of the adjective *imperial*. See Jeanroy, *Poésie lyrique*, I, 113, 152; cf. Avalle, *Peire Vidal*, Nos. 10.10, 15.10, 17.30, and 18.19. Other stories about Peire have influenced later writers; the tale about Peire disguising himself as a wolf to woo his Lady Loba ("She-Wolf") is mentioned by Pound in Canto 14 (see Introduction).

79. PEIROL

Peirol was a poor knight of Auvergne from a castle named Peirol[1] which is in the region of the Dalfin,[2] at the foot of Rochefort.[3] And he was a courtly man and handsome in appearance. And the Dalfin of Auvergne kept Peirol with him and clothed him and gave him horses and arms.

And the Dalfin had a sister named Sail de Claustra,[4] beautiful and good and well regarded, who was the wife of Lord Béraut de Mercoeur, a great baron of Auvergne. Lord Peirol loved her truly, and the Dalfin wooed her for him and was very pleased with the songs Peirol composed about his sister.[5]

The Dalfin knew well how to make them please his sister, so that the lady loved Peirol and gave him the pleasure of love with the knowledge of the Dalfin.

And the love of the lady and Peirol grew so much that the Dalfin became jealous of her, for he believed that she accorded the poet more than was appropriate. And he parted with Peirol and banished him and did not clothe him or arm him. So Peirol was unable to maintain himself as a knight and became a minstrel. And he went around the courts and received clothing and money and horses from the barons.

[1] Either Pérols, in the commune of Prondines, arrondissement of Clermont-Ferrand, or less likely, Pérol, in the commune of Saint-Priest-des-Champs, arrondissement of Riom (Cantal), now called Riom-es-Montagnes.
[2] Dauphin d'Auvergne. See Vida 27.
[3] Rochefort-Montagne, in the arrondissement of Clermont-Ferrand (Puy-de-Dôme).
[4] Sail de Claustra (meaning "escaped from the cloister") was the wife of Béraut III from Mercoeur, near Issoire in Puy-de-Dôme. She is also mentioned in the vida of Guillem de Saint Leidier, 47.
[5] For Peirol's 32 poems, see S. C. Aston's *Peirol, Troubadour of Auvergne* (Cambridge, 1953).

An Album of Troubadour Illuminations
from Manuscripts
(*Courtesy of the Bibliothèque Nationale, Paris*)

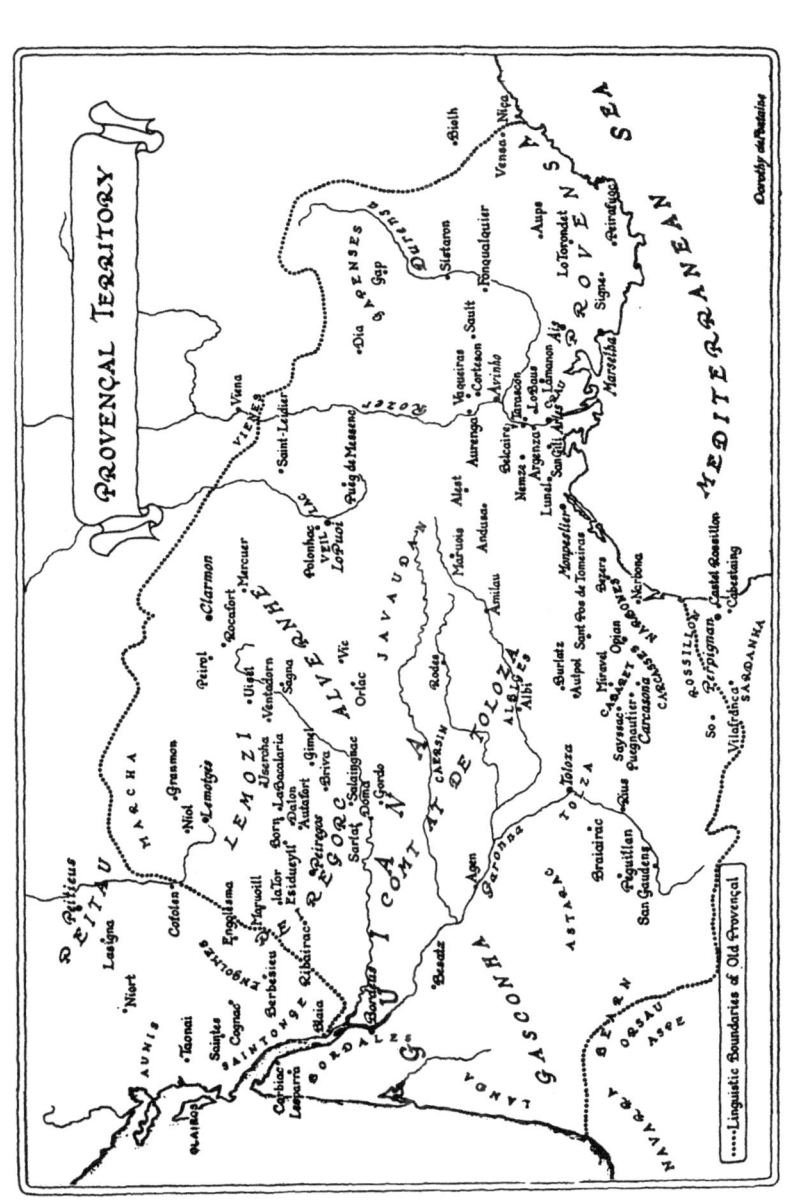

PROVENÇAL TERRITORY

Dorothy de Pontaine

..... Linguistic Boundaries of Old Provençal

Plate 1. The castle of Altafort, now called Hautefort, once the home of Bertran de Born.

Plate 2. The entranceway to the Castle of Excideuil, once the home of Giraut de Borneill.

Plate 3. The Castle of Marueil, once the home of Arnaut de Marueil.

1. ARNAUT DANIEL (B.N. French 12473; folio 50r)

2. BERNART DE VENTADORN (B.N. French 12473; folio 15v)

3. BERTRAN DE BORN (B.N. French 854, folio 174v)

4. BERTRAN DE BORN (B.N. French 12473; folio 160r)

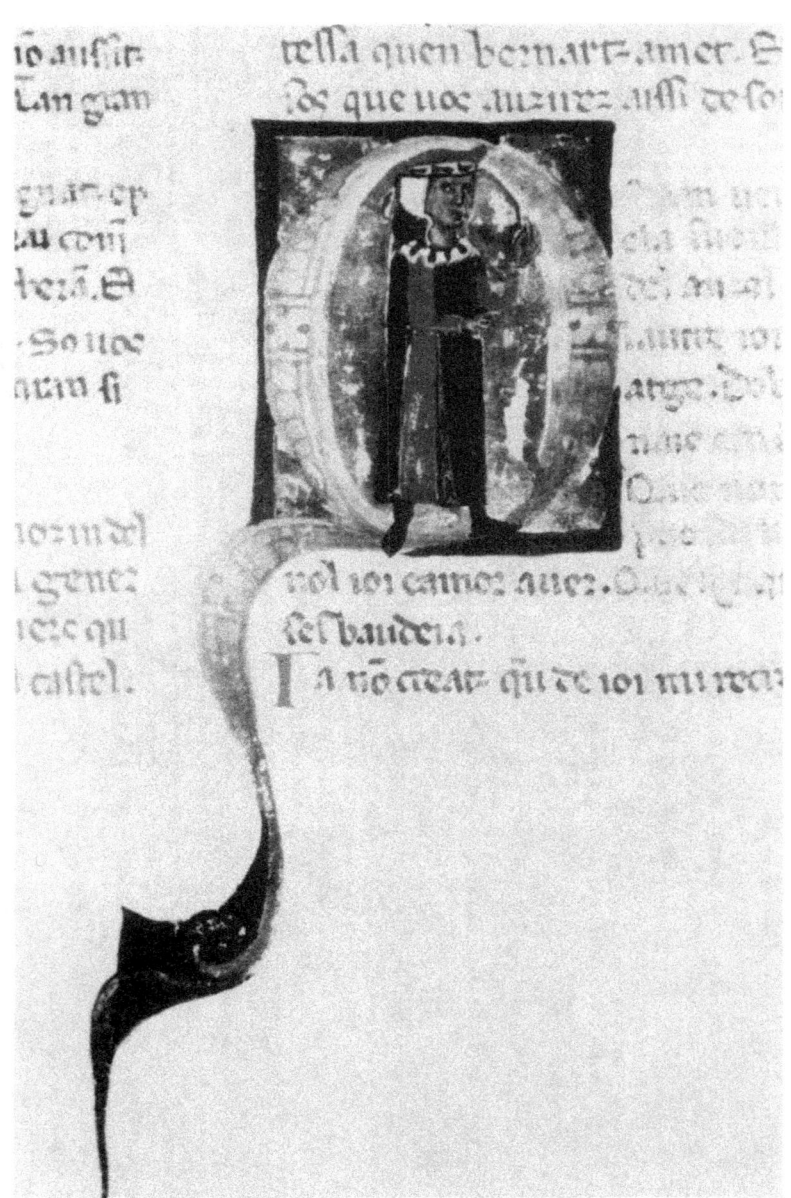

5. BONIFACI CALVO (B.N. French 854; folio 95v)

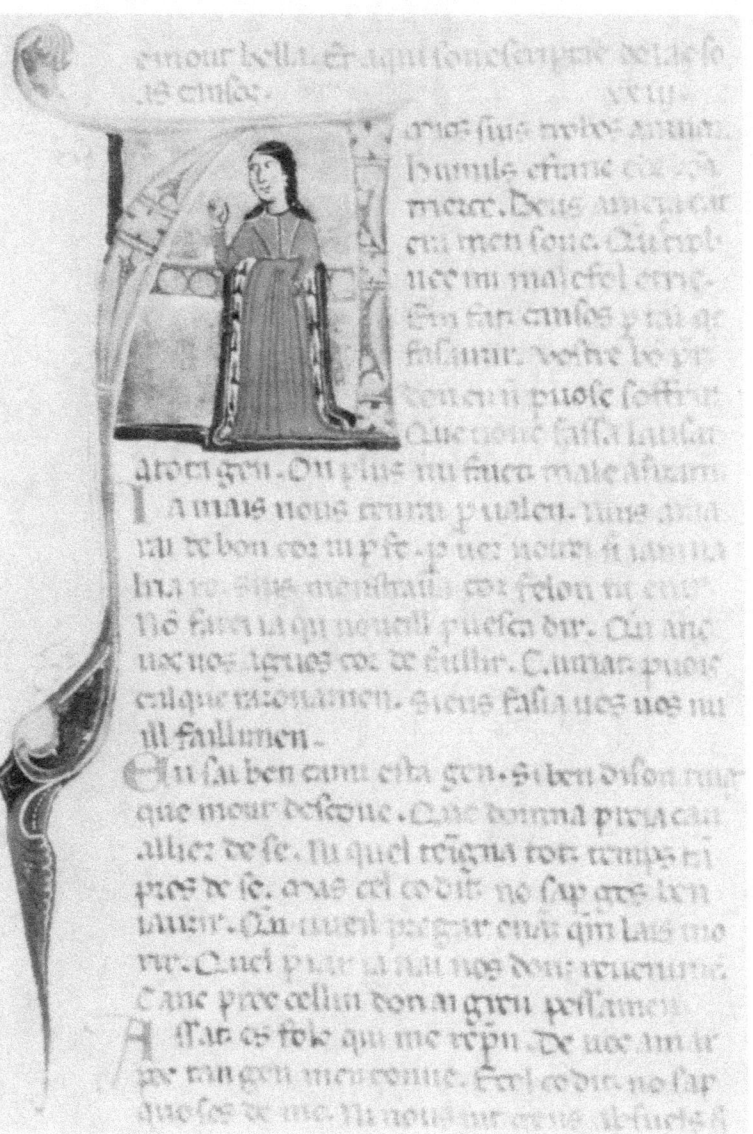

6. LADY CASTELLOZA (B.N. French 12473; folio 110v)

7. CERCAMON (B.N. French 854; folio 133r)

folquer de marseilla.

bor. Oe de nuillautra fec ric
Per quer perbati amoze fo
ufiez poz uas uec nom adire.
ten dan maintas falos. Oe fon
om fo aucc dure. Oeuc aife

8. FOLQUET DE MARSEILLA (B.N. French 12473; folio 46r)

molt boc soe eloe mori. Efer se iogiar. po
caufon quel poer aoc de daz tot son auer. i
jome so que ae gran larguesa. efo molt g
oz de maniar ebe beure. pfo uene gros i
oltra mesura. qolt so longa sasoe deasthu
ce de toe. edonoz aprendze. Que plue de.
xx ane. aner ape p lomon. O-uel ni sac ca
soe nociam grazida ni uolguda. Efi tole
moillez una soldadeza. Quel mener lonce
temps con si p cozte. er auia nom Guillel
ma monia. foz so bella efozt enseingna
da. esi uene si grossa esi grassa con eza el. Er
ella si so dun rie boze que anom Alest. De
la marqua de proensa. Della seingnoria de
bernart dandusa. Emissecre lo marques bo
nisace de mon ferrar. apoe lo en auez. er en
roba. Et en tin gran prete lui esac cansoe.
Gauselm saudize.   XXXIII.

Ant ai sufert longamen
gran affan. O-uee estre
mais que nom na preu
bee. Dorrur p gran tost
eleu sim uolguee. Quala
bella no preua ia doloze.
En que mala foe beuta
p cualoze. Don regarda
part sozsate mon corr
arge. Epoe nom uol se
grau auat marge. Apae lei no cal ni no so
ren Adam. De peidze me nil bendig de mo
chan.

Pero nil ren ren om uil quee p scan. Eral re

9. GAUCELM FAIDIT (B.N. French 854; folio 33v)

ΙΟ. GAUCELM FAIDIT (another portrait) (B.N. French 12473; folio 22r)

11. GUILLEM (WILLIAM) IX OF AQUITAINE, THE COUNT OF POITIERS (B.N. French 854; folio 142v)

12. GIRAUT DE BORNEILL (B.N. French 12473; folio 4r)

13. GUI D'UISEL (B.N. French 854; folio 89v)

14. GUILLEM DE BERGUEDAN (B.N. French 854; folio 192v)

15. GUILLEM MAGRET (B.N. French 854; folio 139r)

16. JAUFRE RUDEL (B.N. French 12473; folio 107v)

17. JORDAN BONEL (left) AND JAUFRE RUDEL (right) (B.N. French 854; folio 121v)

dautra no fo amatz. Troba
muere com se recort. De cu
cautuiez seruetez. fez edis r
nas edamor.

Dires
mens
es qi l
tant r
es. No
finar.
chan
uos de
Alstaz
netar.
Lafin
aue el meus apios. No say tn
Com no li puesca enseignar.
bora es

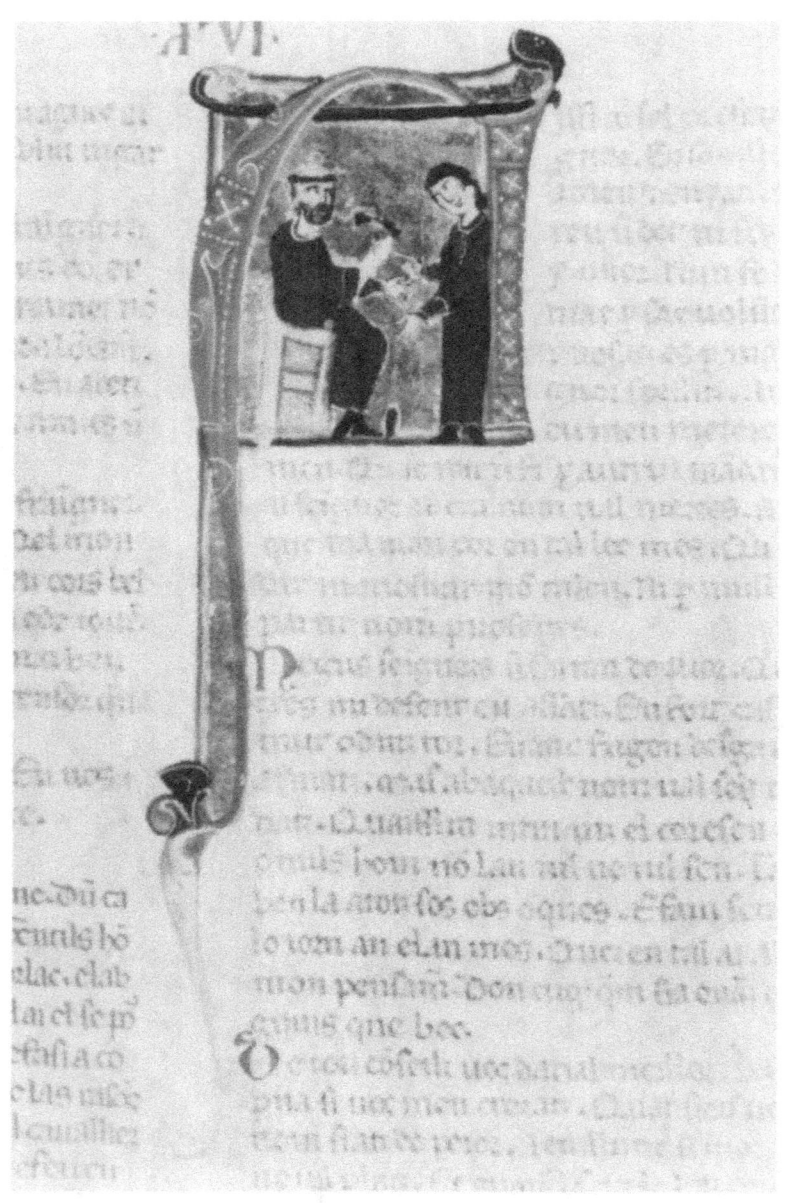

19. LO MONGES DE MONTAUDON or THE MONK OF MON-
TAUDON (B.N. French 854; folio 135r)

20. THE MONK OF MONTAUDON (another portrait) (B.N. French 12473; folio 121r)

21. PEIRE DEL PUOI (left) AND THE KING OF ARAGON (right) (B.N. French 854; folio 108r)

22. PEIRE VIDAL (B.N. French 854; folio 39r)

.anua nom fait Genuas . ʒ aia ſon eſcritas
grauien de las ſoas chanſos.

x̃ v.

En deu en bona cort dm
bon ſoner quill' ʒp qͦ
retraura . on leuer e
qui la pren . ʒparʒ dome
nõ calen . Cauſſi con ſi
nom ealia . fae lengues
ſonen . Quel plue grie
us ſembla q̃ ſia . Dos

eleus ʒp faire

23. PERDIGON (B.N. French 12473; folio 36r)

24. RICHART (RIGAUT) DE BERBEZILL (B.N. French 12473; folio 71r)

25. UC BRUNET (B.N. French 12473; folio 86v)

80. PERDIGON

Part I. All manuscripts

    Perdigon was a minstrel, and he knew how to play the
fiddle well and how to invent poetry.[1] And he was from the
bishopric of Gevaudan[2] from a small town called Lespéron.[3]
And he was the son of a poor man who was a fisherman. And
because of his wit and his inventiveness in poetry he gained
great fame and great honor, so that Dauphin of Auvergne[4]
took him as his knight and clothed him and armed him for a
long time and gave him land and a rent. And all the princes
and the great barons bestowed great honor upon him. And he
enjoyed much good fortune for a long time.

[1] See H. J. Chaytor, *Les Chansons de Perdigon* (Paris,
   1926), for texts of the fourteen surviving lyrics.
[2] Ancient region of *Gabales*, today in Lozère.
[3] Lespéron is the canton of Concouron, arrondissement of
   Largentière (Ardèche).
[4] See Vida 27.

Part II

A. Version of manuscripts *ABIKa*

    But his condition changed greatly. For death took good
fortune away from him and gave him misfortune. For he lost
his men friends and his women friends, and fame and honor
and wealth. And so he entered the order of Cîteaux,[1] and
there he died.

[1] Whether Perdigon ended his life in a Cistercian
   monastery is still open to question. The somber poems
   7 and 8 could have inspired such a conclusion; see E.
   Hoepffner, "La Biographie de Perdigon," *Romania*, *53*
   (1927), 363.

Part II

B. Version of manuscript *E*

And enjoying such honor and such fame, he went with the
Prince of Orange, Lord Guillem des Baux,[1] with Lord Folquet
of Marseille, who was the Bishop of Toulouse,[2] and with the
Abbot of Cîteaux[3] to Rome, seeking to harm the Count of
Toulouse[4] and in order to arrange the crusade. This is why
the good Count Raimon of Toulouse was stripped of his
possessions and his nephew, the Count of Béziers,[5] was
killed. The Toulousain[6] and Quercy[7] and Béziers[8] and the
Albigeois[9] were destroyed. King Pedro of Aragon[10] with a
thousand knights was killed in front of Muret,[11] and twenty
thousand other men were killed. Perdigon brought about and
arranged all these deeds.

And he exhorted the people to take the cross by singing.
And he gave praise to God, because he had humiliated and
killed the King of Aragon, who had clothed him. For this
reason he declined in fame and in honor and in wealth, and
all the worthy men who remained alive held him in contempt
and did not want to see him or hear him. And all the barons
who were his friends were killed by the war: the Count of
Montfort,[12] and Lord Guillem des Baux,[13] and all the
others who had instigated the crusade. And Count Raimon
recovered his land.

Perdigon did not dare to come or to go. And the Dalfin
d'Alvernhe took away all the land and the rent he had given
him. He went away to Lambert of Monteil, who was the
son-in-law of Lord Guillem des Baux,[14] and begged him to
let him enter a house of the Cistercian order called
Silvabela.[15] And he had him received as a monk in the
monastery. And there he ended his days. And here are
written some of his songs.

[1] Guillaume des Baux, Prince of Orange, is confused here
with his brother, Uc des Baux, with whom Perdigo was
acquainted.
[2] See Vida 33.
[3] This account of Perdigo's collaboration with the
anti-Albigensian forces is inaccurate. See E.
Hoepffner, "La Biographie de Perdigon", *Romania, 53*

(1927), 360.

[4] Raimon VI (1194-1222).
[5] Raimon-Roger (1194-1209) was viscount--not count--of Béziers (Hérault).
[6] Region around Toulouse.
[7] The departments of Tarn-et-Garonne and Lot.
[8] Seat of an arrondissement in Hérault.
[9] Region around Albi (Tarn).
[10] Pedro II (1196-1213).
[11] At Muret (Haute-Garonne), Pedro of Aragon did in fact come to the rescue of the Count of Toulouse. But he was defeated and died in the battle.
[12] Simon de Montfort, Count of Leicester, was killed in 1218 at the siege of Toulouse.
[13] Guillem des Baux was massacred by the people of Avignon after the Albigensian crusade (1218).
[14] Lambert of Monteil was not the son-in-law of William of Orange (Chaytor, p. vi.)
[15] "Beautiful Forest," a Cistertian abbey that never existed. See Hoepffner, "Biographie," p. 363.

81. PISTOLETA

Pistoleta[1] was a singer of Lord Arnaut de Maruoill[2] and was from Provence. And later he became an inventor of poetry and composed songs with graceful melodies. And he was well esteemed among high society. But he was a man who was not given to conversation and was of poor appearance and slight worth. And he took a wife in Marseille and became a merchant. And he became rich and stopped going around the courts. And he composed these songs.

[1] According to E. Niestroy, *Der trobador Pistoleta* (Halle, 1914), p. 7, Pistoleta could have received this nickname ("Little letter") because of his occupation as a messenger of love between Arnaut de Marueil and the Countess of Burlatz.

[2] See Vida 11.

82. PONS DE CAPDOILL

Pons de Capdoill[1] was from the same bishopric as Guilhem de Saint Leidier.[2] He was a rich man and a very noble baron. And he knew well how to invent poetry and how to play the fiddle and sing. He was a very capable knight, eloquent, a gracious wooer of ladies, tall and handsome, and very learned, and greatly lacking in possessions. But he disguised this by graciously welcoming and personally honoring others.

And he truly loved Lady Azalais de Mercoeur,[3] the wife of Lord Oisil de Mercoeur,[4] who was the daughter of Lord Bernart d'Anduze, an honored baron from the march of Provence. He loved her greatly and praised her and composed many good songs about her. And as long as she lived, he never loved another woman. And when she died, he took the cross and went overseas, and there he died. And here are written a great number of his songs.

[1] Capdoill is today Saint-Julien-Chapteuil, in the arrondissement of Le Puy. Pons was the lord of Vertaison, in the arrondissement of Clermont-Ferrand (S. Stronski, "Recherches," 483-485.) For Pons' 26 poems, see the only edition: M. von Napolski, *Leben und Werke des Trobadors Pons de Capduoill* (Halle, 1879).

[2] See Vida 47.

[3] Daughter of Bernart VII of Anduze. Mercoeur is probably in the arrondissement of Brioude (Haute-Loire).

[4] The identity of Odilon de Mercoeur is unknown.

83. RAIMBAUT D'AURENGA (OF ORANGE)

Raimbaut d'Aurenga was the lord of Orange[1] and of
Courthézon[2] and of many other castles. And he was able and
learned and a capable knight and an eloquent speaker. And
he delighted in honorable ladies and in honorable gallantry.
And he was a good inventor of poems and of songs, but he was
most intent on making difficult and subtle rhymes. And he
loved for a long time a lady from Provence whose name was
Maria de Vertfuoil,[3] and he called her his "Joglar"[4] in
his songs. He loved her for a long time and she loved him.
And he composed many good songs about her and [did] many
other good deeds.

And he fell in love afterwards with the good Countess of
Urgel,[5] who was a Lombard, daughter of the Marquis of
Busca.[6] She was very honored and esteemed above all the
noble ladies of Urgel. And Raimbaut, without seeing her, by
the great good that he heard spoken of her, fell in love
with the countess, and she with him. And he also composed
songs about her, and he sent her his songs with a minstrel
named Rossignol,[7] as he says in a song:

My friend Nightingale,
Though you are full of grief,
For my sake, rejoice
Through a lively little song
Which you will carry without delay
To the noble countess,
There in Urgel, as a present.[8]

He was in love with this countess for a long time, and he
loved her without seeing her. And he never had the courage
to go and see her. This is why I heard her say, when she
was already a nun, that, if he had come, she would have
given him pleasure by allowing him to touch her naked leg
with the back of his hand. Loving her in this way, Raimbaut
died without a male heir, and Orange was left to his two
daughters. One of them was the wife of the Lord of Agout;
from the other were born Lord Uc des Baux and Lord Guillem
des Baux. And the first was the mother of Guillem d'Orange,
who died young and in a bad way, and of Raimbaut, who gave
half of the city of Orange to the Hospital.[9]

[1] Seat of a canton in the arrondissement of Avignon (Vaucluse).

[2] In the arrondissement of Avignon (Vaucluse).

[3] Maria de Vertfuoil, together with the Countess of Urgel (note 6), are fictional lovers of Raimbaut. See W. T. Pattison, *The Life and Works of the Troubadour Raimbaut d'Orange* (Minneapolis, 1952), pp. 7-30, for a full account of the poet's life and for Raimbaut's 41 poems.

[4] "Jongleur"; a frequent *senhal* in Raimbaut's poetry. For details, see Pattison; A. Sakari, "Azalais de Porcairagues," 23-43.

[5] Countess of Urgel, another of the poet's fictional lovers. Urgel, now in Catalonia, was then part of the kingdom of Aragon.

[6] Probably Ermengaud X.

[7] Nightingale. Nothing is known about this jongleur.

[8] Amics Rossignol,
Si tot as gran dol
Per la mi'amor t'esjau
Ab una leu chanzoneta
Qe.m portaras a jornau
A la contessa valen
Lai en U[r]gel per presen (Boutière-Schutz, p. 442)
These verses appear only in one manuscript and probably belong to a lost poem. Kolsen proposed that they might be a variant to the second *tornada* of 389.17, but the meters of the two poems are not compatible (A. Kolsen, *Guiraut de Borneill*, p. 63).

[9] Raimbaut died, in fact, in Courthézon in 1173. He left no heirs and willed his property to his two sisters Tiburgette and Tiburge (mother of Guillem, who was quartered by the people of Avignon for his role in the Crusade, and Uc des Baux). Raimbaut VI, the poet's great-nephew (not grandson) gave half of the city of Orange to the Order of the Frères Hospitaliers in 1215. See Pattison, pp. 25-30, 218-219 (containing the text of Raimbaut's will).

84. RAIMBAUT DE VAQUEIRAS

A. Version of all manuscripts

Raimbaut de Vaqueiras was the son of a poor knight of
Provence from the castle of Vaqueiras,[1] who was called
Peirol and was thought to be mad. Lord Raimbaut became a
minstrel and spent a long time with the Prince of Orange,
Guillem des Baux.[2] He knew how to sing well and how to
compose couplets and *sirventes*. And the Prince of Orange
did him much good and honored him greatly, and he increased
his rank and made him known and esteemed among high society.

And Raimbaut came to Montferrat,[3] to my lord the Marquis
Bonifaci.[4] And he was in his court for a long time. And he
improved in wit and in arms and in invention. And he fell
in love with the sister of the Marquis, who was called Lady
Beatrice[5] and was the wife of Enrico del Carretto,[6] and he
invented many good songs about her. And he called her "Bels
Cavalliers"[7] in his songs. And it was believed that she
truly loved him. And when the marquis went over to
Romania,[8] he took Raimbaut with him and made him a knight.
And he gave him much land and a large rent in the kingdom of
Thessalonika.[9] And there he died.

[1] Vaqueiras is in the canton of Beaumes, arrondissement
of Orange (Vaucluse).

[2] The sequence of events in the text may be wrong (see
Vida 51). Jeanroy believes that Raimbaut's relation
with Boniface precedes his stay with Guillem (*Poésie
lyrique*, I, 233).

[3] Region in Italy, between the Piedmont region of Milan,
and the Republic of Genoa, including much of
present-day Alessandria and Acqui.

[4] Boniface of Montferrat (ca. 1152-1207) was the son of
William III of Montferrat. He became governor of the
marquisate in 1183 and inherited the title to it in
1192. His relation with Raimbaut probably dates from
1175 (see Jeanroy, *Poésie lyrique*, I, 231.)

[5] None of Boniface's sisters was called Béatrice. This
probably refers to his daughter.

[6] Enrico del Carretto (known 1181-1231), marquis of Noli
and of Finale, may have been married to Boniface's
daughter.

[7] "Bel Cavalier [Fair Knight] was undoubtedly a lady of high rank living at the court of Montferrat." See J. Linskill, *The Poems of the Troubadour Raimbaut de Vaqueiras* (The Hague, 1964), p. 24.

[8] The Byzantine Empire. Raimbaut went to Constantinople with the marquis in 1202. Earlier (1194-95) he had fought at his side in Sicily.

[9] Boniface, a leader of the Fourth Crusade, received the kingdom of Thessalonika, now Salonika in northern Greece, in 1204.

B. Interpolation of manuscript *P*, and
    Razo of P.-C. 392.20 and 392.24.

Raimbaut de Vaqueiras was from a castle called Vaqueiras, and he was the son of a poor knight called Peirol, who was thought to be mad. And Raimbaut became a minstrel and spent a long time with the Prince of Orange, called Guillem des Baux. He knew how to sing well and how to compose couplets and *sirventes*. And the Prince of Orange did him great good and great honor and enhanced his position and made him known and esteemed among high society.

And he came to Montferrat to the Marquis Boniface. And he stayed with him for a long time, and he increased in arms and in invention so that he enjoyed great fame in the court. And the marquis, because of the great worth he recognized in him, made him a knight and his comrade in arms and in belongings. So he fell in love with the sister of the marquis, who was called Lady Beatrice and was the wife of Enrico del Carretto. And he invented many good songs about her. And he called her "Bel Cavalier."

And this is why he called her this: Lord Raimbaut had such good fortune that he could see Lady Beatrice whenever he wanted, as long as she was in her room, through a keyhole. Nobody noticed this. And one day the marquis came in from the hunt. And he entered the room and put his sword next to the bed and went out. And Lady Beatrice stayed in the room and took off her mantle and remained in her coat. And she took the sword and girt it in the manner of a knight. And she took it out of its sheath and brandished it up high and swung it in her hand from one side to the other. And she put it back in the sheath, ungirded it, and put it back by the side of the bed. And Lord Raimbaut de Vaqueiras saw everything I told you through the keyhole. So for this reason he afterwards called her "Bel Cavalier" in his songs, as he says in the first couplet of this song which begins this way:

> I never thought to see the day when love should so dominate me that a lady would hold me completely in her power, for I would show myself haughty to match their haughtiness, as is my wont, but beauty and youth and a gracious, delightful presence and the lively, pleasing discourse of my Fair Knight have tamed my wildness. And the hard-hearted man, after he relents towards love before an object who is precious, shows more art in loving his lady than a man of gentle disposition who loves immoderately and without discrimination.[1]

And it was believed that she truly loved him. And in this way he stayed with the marquis for a long time and had much happiness with him. When the marquis went over to Romania, he took Lord Raimbaut de Vaqueiras with him. So he felt great sadness for the love of his lady, who remained over here among us. And he himself would have remained gladly, but because of his appreciation of the marquis for the great honor he had received from him, he did not dare refuse to go. And so he went with him. But at all times he strove to be valiant at arms, and to be worthy in war and in all praiseworthy good deeds. And he acquired great honor and great wealth. But in spite of all this he did not forget his sadness, as he says in the fourth couplet of the song which begins:

Neither winter nor spring delights me[2]

and the strophe says:

> What then are conquest and riches to me? For I thought myself richer when I was a faithful lover and was loved, and had my fill of love, my lord *Engles*; then, only one gracious gesture charmed me

91

more than great lands and great possessions; for
ever as my power grows, so my own displeasure with
myself is greater, since my beloved Fair Knight
and joy are far from me and have fled; thus I will
no longer be comforted, and so my sadness is
greater and more burdensome.[3]

And Raimbaut de Vaqueiras lived like this, as you have
heard. And he showed a better appearance than his heart
inspired him to. And he had great suzerainty which the
marquis had given him in the kingdom of Thessalonika. And
there he died.

[1] Ja non cuidei vezer
C'Amor me destrenses
Tan qe dopna[.m] tengues
Del tot en son poder;
Qe contra lor orgueill
For' orgoilhos con s[u]eil;
Mas beutat et jovenz,
E.l gentilz cors plagenz
E.ill gai ditz plasenti[er]
De mon Bel Cavalier
M'a[n] fait privat d'estraing;
E puois dur cor s'afraing
Vas Amor, en loc car,
Sap mielz sa dompna amar
C'umilz trop amoros,
De totas envejos (P.-C. 392.20). (Translation from
Linskill, p. 178.)

[2] No m'agrad'iver[n]s ni pascors

[3] Donc qe.m val conqis[tz] ni ricors?
Q'eu ja.m tenia per plus rics,
Qant er' amatz et fins amics
E.m pa[i]ssia, N' E[n]gles, Amors;
N'amava mais un sol plaser
Qe sai grant cort et grant aver;
C'ades, on plus mes poders creis,
Ai major ir' ab mi meseis,
Pois mos Bels Cavaliers grasit[z]
Et jois m'es lo[n]iatz et fugitz;
Do[n] mais no.m naisera conortz,
Per q'es magier l'ir et plus fortz. (P.-C. 392.24)

85.   RAIMON DE DURFORT and TURC MALEC

Raimon de Durfort[1] and Lord Turc Malec[2] were two
knights from Quercy[3] who composed the *sirventes* about the
lady called Milady Aia,[4] the one who said to the knight of
Cornil[5] that she would not love him if he did not blow in
her arse.   And here are written the *sirventes*.

[1] Durfort is in the canton of Luzerte, arrondissement of
  Moissac (Tarn-et-Garonne).
[2] Also named *Truc* and *Malet* in different chansonniers.
[3] Now the departments of Tarn-et-Garonne and Lot.
[4] Unknown lady whose name appears in various forms in
  the manuscripts.
[5] Bernart de Cornil, according to two *sirventes* (P.-C.
  397.1 and 447.1) of Raimon and Turc.   There is a town
  of Cornil in the canton of Tulle (Corrèze).   More
  likely, however, the name is related to *cornar*,
  obvious subject of the anecdote.

86.   RAIMON JORDAN

A.   Version of manuscript *R*

Raimon Jordan was viscount of Saint Antonin,[1] and lord
of a rich town in Quercy.   And he was charming and generous
and able at arms, and he knew how to invent poetry and how
to create well.[2]   And he loved the wife of Lord R. Amielh de
Pena d'Albigeois,[3] who was an honorable baron.   And the
lady was beautiful, and young, and learned, and she loved
the viscount more than anything in the world, and he
likewise loved her.

And it came to pass that the viscount was at war with his
enemies, and he was wounded in battle and taken to Saint
Antonin as if he were dead.   And the news reached the lady

93

that he was dead. She felt such grief at this that she entered the order of the Patarins.[4] The viscount recovered from his wound, but when he learned that the lady had entered a monastery, he felt such grief that he never again composed poems or songs. And here you have some of his works.

[1] In the arrondissement of Montauban (Tarn-et-Garonne).
[2] For texts of the eleven poems, see H. Kjellman, *Le Troubadour Raimon Jordan, vicomte de Saint-Antonin* (Uppsala, 1922).
[3] R. Amiel de Penne d'Albigeois, possibly confused with R. Amielz de Penne, mentioned in a document of 1198. Penne is in the canton of Vaour, arrondissement of Gaillac (Tarn).
[4] *Patarics* ("heretics"), Cathars, Albigensians.

B. Version of manuscripts *ABIK*, and *Razo of P.-C. 404.9 and 404.12.*

The viscount of Saint Antonin was from the bishopric of Cahors,[1] lord and viscount of Saint Antonin. And he loved a noble lady who was the wife of the lord of Pena d'Albigeois, from a rich and powerful castle. The lady was noble and beautiful and worthy and highly esteemed and highly honored; and he was very worthy and learned and able at arms and handsome and a good inventor of poetry, and his name was Raimon Jordan. The lady was called the Viscountess of Pena.

The love of both was without bounds, so much they loved one another. And it so happened that the viscount went into the region of his enemies wearing his armor, and there ensued a great battle, and the viscount was mortally wounded. And his enemies announced his death; and the news reached the lady that he had died, and she, because of the great sadness and the great pain which she felt at this news, left at once and joined the order of the heretics. And as God willed it, the viscount was healed and he recovered from the wound. And no one wanted to tell him that she had entered the convent.

And when he was fully recovered, he went to Saint Antonin, and they told him how she had entered the order because of the sadness she felt when she was told that he had died. So when he heard this, he lost joy and laughter and song and happiness; he turned to lamentation and weeping and sighing and dismay and pain, and he did not ride on horseback or come or go among high society. And so he spent more than a year in great affliction.

Then Lady Elis de Monfort,[2] wife of Lord Guillem de Gordon and daughter of the Viscount of Turenne,[3] endowed with youth and beauty and courtesy and worth, sent for him with many gracious entreaties, that he should let himself be cheered by her love and leave the pain and sadness which afflicted him, saying that she would give him her heart and her body and her love in compensation for the unhappiness he had suffered. And begging him and asking him to please deign to come and see her, and if not, that she be permitted to come and see him.

When the viscount heard these honorable and flattering messages which the noble worthy lady was sending him, he began to feel a great sweetness of love come to his heart, so that he began to feel happiness and to enjoy himself, and he began to come to town, and to rediscover joy among high society, and to dress himself and his companions, and to furnish himself with equipment and arms and pleasant company. And he prepared himself well and honorably, and he went to my lady Elis de Monfort, and she received him with great pleasure and with great honor.

And he was pleased and happy with the honor and the pleasure which she gave him in word and deed, and she was very happy with the goodness and the worth and the wit and the knowledge and the courtesy which she found in him. And she did not regret the gracious and loving [messages] which she had sent him. And he knew well how to praise her and how to thank her, and how to woo her in a charming way in order that she might show him enough love to make him believe that she had sent him the gracious messages with noble sentiment and in good faith. He carried them, he said, engraved in the depths of this heart. And she did well, for she took him as her knight and received his homage, and she gave herself to him as his lady, kissing and embracing, and gave him the ring from her finger as a token.

And so the viscount left her very happy and very pleased, and he turned again to inventing poetry and singing and joy. And so he composed about her that song which says:

I beg of you, to whom I have entrusted
my love.[4]

And before he composed this song, one night as he slept it seemed to him that Love addressed to him a couplet which says:

Raimon Jordan, from you yourself I wish
to learn
How you abandoned pleasure and singing.
In the past you used to understand gallantry
Very loyally, or so it seemed,
And you feigned and pretended to be gay.
But now I see you have finished the melody;
You are at fault if no one will defend you.[5]

He composed many good songs, some of which are written here, as you will hear.

[1] Seat of the department of Lot.
[2] Lady whose identity confuses modern critics and medieval biographers alike. See Boutière-Schutz, p. 166.
[3] In the arrondissement of Brive-la-Gaillarde (Corrèze).
[4] Vas vos soplei, en cui ai mes m'entenssa. (P.-C. 404.12)
[5] Raimonz Jordanz, de vos eis voill aprendre
Co.us es laissatz de solatz e de chan.
Ja soliatz en dompnejar entendre
Molt leialmen, so fasiatz semblan
E.us feiniatz, e.us en fasiatz gais
Mas ara vei c'avetz fenit lo lais
Encolpatz etz, se non es qu'i responda. (P.-C. 404.9)

87. RAIMON DE MIRAVAL

Raimon de Miraval was a poor knight from Carcassès[1] who did not have more than a quarter of the castle of Miraval.[2] And in that castle there were hardly forty men. But because of his beautiful inventions and his beautiful discourse, and because he knew more about love and gallantry and all gracious deeds and pleasing discourse common among lovers and their mistresses, he was greatly honored and esteemed by the Count of Toulouse.[3] And they called one another "Audiartz."[4] And the count gave him the horses and the arms and the clothing that he needed. And he influenced the count and his house, as well as King Pedro of Aragon[5] and the Viscount of Béziers[6] and Lord Bertran de Saissac[7] and all the great barons of that region.

And there was no great or worthy lady in that entire region who did not desire and did not take pains to be courted by him or to love him privately, for he knew better than any other man how to honor them and how to praise them. So that none of them considered herself esteemed if Raimon de Miraval was not her friend. He courted many ladies and composed many good songs about them. And it was believed that he never received anything in the realm of love from any of them, and that they all deceived him. He ended his life in Lérida in the convent of Sancta Clara, of the sisters of Cîteaux.[8]

---

[1] Region around Carcassonne (Aude).
[2] Miraval-Cabardès, in the canton of Mas-Cabardès, arrondissement of Carcassonne (Aude).
[3] Raimon VI, count of Toulouse (1194-1222).
[4] This woman's name, Hildegarde, appears sixteen times as a *senhal* in Miraval's poems. Cf. the reciprocal *senhal* mentioned in Vida 51. See L. T. Topsfield, *Les Poésies du Troubadour Raimon de Miraval* (Paris, 1971) for Raimon's 44 poems.
[5] Pedro II of Aragon (1196-1213).
[6] Roger II (1167-1194) or Raimon-Roger (1194-1209).
[7] Bertran de Saissac was counselor to the viscount of Béziers. Saissac is in the arrondissement of Carcassonne.
[8] This sentence occurs only in manuscript *E*. Whether Raimon did end his life in the Cistercian nunnery of

Santa Clara in Lérida (Catalonia, Spain) is not known.
See P. Andraud, *La Vie et l'oeuvre de Raimon de
Miraval* (Paris, 1902), p. 25.

87. RAIMON DE LAS SALAS

Raimon de Salas[1] was a burgher from Marseille. And he
invented songs and dawn songs and *retroensas*.[2] He was not
very well known or esteemed.

[1] More commonly referred to as Raimon de las Salas or
Raimon de la Sala. See his four poems in F. M.
Chambers, "Raimon de las Salas", *Essays in Honor of
Louis Francis Solano* (Chapel Hill, 1970), 29-51.
[2] Raimon and Ferrari de Ferrara (see Vida 32) are the
only troubadours to whom this genre is attributed.
The oldest known *retroensa* [see Glossary] is a French
crusade song of 1146-1147; others talk of love and celebrate the Virgin. See Boutière-Schutz, pp. 510-511,
for a more detailed discussion of the genre.

89. RAINAUT and JAUFRE DE PONS

Rainaut de Pons[1] was a noble castellan from Saintonge,[2]
from the march of Poitou, and he was lord of the castle of
Pons. He knew how to invent poetry. And Lord Jaufre de
Pons was a gentleman of the castle, and he also knew how to
invent poetry, and he composed *tensos* with Rainaut de Pons.

[1] In the arrondissement of Saintes (Charente-Maritime).
[2] Region in the West of France (Charente-Maritime).

[2] Region in the West of France (Charente-Maritime).

90.   RICAU (RICHAUT) DE TARASCON

Richaut de Tarascon was a knight from Provence, from the castle of Tarascon.[1] He was a good knight and a good inventor of poetry and a good servant [of ladies]. And he composed good *sirventes* and good songs.

[1] Seat of a canton in the arrondissement of Arles (Bouches-du-Rhône). Two poems survive, unedited.

91.   RICHART DE BERBEZILL (RIGAUT DE BERBEZILH, BARBEZIEUX)

Richart de Berbezill[1] was a knight from the castle of Barbezieux in Saintonge[2] in the bishopric of Saintes, a poor minor noble. He was a capable knight and handsome in appearance. And he knew better how to compose poetry than to listen[3] to it or recite it. He was a very timid speaker in public, and the more noble people he saw, the more he was troubled and the less he knew. And he always needed someone to encourage him. But he sang and he executed melodies in a charming way.

And he fell in love with a lady, wife of Lord Jaufre of Tonnay,[4] a worthy baron of that region. And the lady was noble and beautiful and gay and charming and very desirous of merit and honor, daughter of Lord Jaufre Rudel, the Prince of Blaye.[5]

And when she learned that he was in love with her, she made sweet pretenses of love to him, so much that he summoned up courage to woo her. And she, with sweet pretenses of love, welcomed his requests, received them, and heard them like a lady who desired that a troubadour invent poems about her. And he began to compose songs about her, and he called her "Miellz-de-Domna"[6] in his songs.

And he also took great delight in making in his songs comparisons with animals and birds and men, and with the sun and stars, in order to treat more novel subjects than anyone else had done. He sang about her for a very long time, but it was believed that she never made love with him. And the lady died, and he went away to Spain, to the worthy baron Don Diego.[7] And there he lived and died.

[1] Barbezieux is in the arrondissment of Cognac (Charente).

[2] Province north of Gironde.

[3] *Saup mielhs trobar qu'entendre ni que dire*: Boutière-Schutz translates as "il sut mieux 'trouver' qu'imaginer(?) et dire." Although Schutz has described a specifically aesthetic and technical sense for "entendre" when coupled with "trobar", ("A preliminary study," 129-132), here "entendre" is related to "dire". Hence a more literal meaning ("to hear") seems implied.

[4] Probably Gaufridus de Tonai; today Tonnay-Charente, in the arrondissement of Rochefort (Charente-Maritime).

[5] Jaufre Rudel (see Vida 60) could have had a daughter of marriageable age by 1147. His name, however, appears in only two manuscripts of this text.

[6] *Senhal* meaning "Best of Ladies" that appears in at least four of Richart's poems. See A. Varvaro, *Rigaut de Berbezilh*: *Liriche* (Bari, 1960) and M. Braccini, *Rigaut de Barbezieux*: *Le canzoni, testo e commento* (Florence, 1960) for critical editions of Richart's nine poems.

[7] Diego Lopez Díaz de Haro (a city in Biscay), who died in 1214, was a well known Spanish patron of troubadours. Aimeric de Peguillan (see Vida 3) is known to have sojourned in his court. His name again appears in only two manuscripts.

92. SAIL D'ESCOLA

Sail d'Escola[1] was from Bergerac[2] from a rich town in Perigord, son of a merchant. And he became a minstrel and composed good little songs, and he lived with Lady Ainermada de Narbona.[3] And when she died, he entered the cloister at Bergerac and abandoned inventing and singing.

[1] There have been several interpretations of this troubadour's nickname, among them "Saute-de-Cloître," "transfuge de l'école" and "pédant." See Boutière-Schutz, p. 64, note 1.

[2] Also known as Bragairac, this city is the seat of an arrondissement in Dordogne.

[3] Probably Ermengarde of Narbonne, who died in 1197.

93. SAVARIC DE MAULEON (MALLEO)

Savaric de Mauleon[1] was a rich baron of Poitou, son of Lord Reol de Mauleon.[2] He was the lord of Mauleon and of Talarnom[3] and of Fontenay[4] and of Châtelaillon[5] and of Bouhet[6] and of Benon[7] and of Saint-Michel-en-l'Herme[8] and of the island of Ré[9] and of the island of Nives[10] and of Nestrine[11] and of Angolins[12] and of many other good places.

He was a handsome knight and courtly and learned, and the most generous of generous men. He enjoyed generosity and gallantry and love and tournaments more than anyone in the world, and song and conversation and invention of poetry and courts and munificence. He was the truest lover of ladies and of lovers among all gentlemen, and the most eager to meet good men and to be pleasing to them. And he was the best warrior there ever was. Sometimes he was fortunate in battle, sometimes he encountered misfortune. And all the wars he waged were against the King of France[13] and against his people.

101

And about his good deeds one could write a large book, whoever wanted to write it. For he possessed more humility and grace and sincerity and performed more good deeds than anyone I have ever seen or heard of, and he had the desire to do even more.

[1] Mauleon, since 1736 called Chatillon-sur-Sèvre, in the arrondissement of Bressuire (Deux-Sèvres). For Savaric's two *partimens* and *cobla* see H. J. Chaytor, *Savaric de Mauleon, Baron and Troubadour* (Cambridge, Eng., 1939).

[2] Raoul de Mauleon, Lord of Châtelaillon, was a favorite of Henry II, who gave him possession of the Talmondais (now Talmont) in the arrondissement of Sables-d'Olonne (Vendée).

[3] Probably the region of Talmont.

[4] Fontenay-le-Comte, seat of an arrondissement in Vendée.

[5] Today Châtelaillon-Plage, in the arrondissement of La Rochelle (Charente-Maritime).

[6] In the canton of Aigrefeuille, arrondissement of Rochefort (Charente-Maritime).

[7] In the canton of Courçon, arrondissement of La Rochelle (Charente-Maritime).

[8] In the arrondissement of Fontenay-le-Comte (Vendée).

[9] Dependence of the Charente-Maritime.

[10] Probably the island of Yeu. The name has been considerably altered in the text.

[11] Chabaneau (*Biographies*, p. 47) proposed reading Nestrive--a contamination of two place names near the mouth of the Charente: Nestre and Yves.

[12] In the arrondissement of La Rochelle (Charente-Maritime).

[13] Savaric did not fight against the King of France; however, he played an important political role as seneschal of Aquitaine from 1213 until his death in 1231.

94. SORDEL (SORDELLO)

A. Version of manuscripts *IK*

Sordel[1] was from Sirier de Mantoana,[2] son of a poor knight called Milord El Cort.[3] And he took delight in learning songs and in inventing poetry. And he frequented the notable men of the court and learned all that he could. And he composed couplets and *sirventes*. And he came to the court of the Count of San Bonifacio,[4] and the count honored him greatly. And he fell in love with the wife of the count, but he did so in jest. And she fell in love with him. And it happened that the count was on bad terms with her brothers, so that the count parted with her. And Lord Ezzelin and Lord Alberico,[5] her brothers, had her abducted from the count by Milord Sordel. And he came to be with them, and he stayed with them for a long time in great happiness. And later he went to Provence, where he received great honors from all the notable men, and from the count and the countess[6] who gave him a good castle and a noble wife.

[1] In Italian, Sordello, famous as the guardian of the Vale of Princes in Dante's *Purgatory* 6 and the subject of Robert Browning's long poem *Sordello*. He figures prominently in Ezra Pound's *Cantos*: Canto 2, 6, 29, 36, etc.

[2] Either Cereda (local pronunciation, Serida) or Sereno (local pronunciation, Serino) in the region of Mantua, Italy.

[3] "The short one." *Curtus* was a very common name in the 12th century, particularly in northern Italy. For further biographical details and Sordel's 42 poems, see M. Boni, *Sordello: Le Poesie* (Bologna, 1954).

[4] Rizzardo di San Bonifacio from Verona had married Cunizza, daughter of Ezzelino II da Romano in 1222. She was the sister of Ezzelino III, the tyrant mentioned in Dante's *Inferno* 12, 109-110.

[5] Ezzelino III and Alberico da Romano, a town (near Padua). Alberico was a poet as well as patron of troubadours.

[6] Raimon-Bérengar IV. His wife is either Beatrice of Savoy or Guida of Rodez.

B. Version of manuscripts *Aa*

Sordel was from Mantoana,[1] from a castle called Goito,[2] and was a noble castellan. And he was a charming man in appearance, and was a good singer and a good inventor of poetry, and a great lover. But he was very treacherous toward ladies and toward the barons with whom he lived. And he loved Milady Cunizza,[3] sister of Lord Ezzelino and of Lord Alberico de Romano, who was wife of the Count of San Bonifacio,[4] with whom Sordel lived.

And under orders of Lord Ezzelino he stole Lady Cunizza, and took her away. And shortly thereafter, he went to Cenedes,[5] to a castle of the Estras[6] belonging to Lord Enrico and Lord Guglielmo and Lord Valpertino, who were his very good friends. And he secretly married one of their sisters, called Otta.[7] And afterwards, he went to Treviso. And when the Lord of Estras learned this, he wished to harm him personally, as did the friends of the Count of San Bonifacio. So he stayed armed in the house of Milord Ezzelino. And when he travelled by land, he rode a good charger with a great escort of knights.

And out of fear of those who sought to harm him, he left and went to Provence. And he stayed with the Count of Provence.[8] And he loved a noble and beautiful lady from Provence. And he called her "Doussa-Enemia"[9] in the songs which he composed for her. For this lady he composed many good songs.

---

[1] Mantua, in Italy.

[2] In the northwestern region of Mantua.

[3] Cunizza, daughter of Ezzelino II da Romano, appears with Folquet de Marseille in *Paradiso* 9; she is in Pound's Cantos 6 and 29. Sordello appears in Cantos 6 and 36.

[4] Rizzardo di San Bonifacio, whom Cunizza married in 1222.

[5] Region of Ceneda, north of Treviso (Venetia).

[6] The three lords of Strasso were family friends of the Da Romanos. See Boni, *Sordello*, pp. xxxviii-xxxix.

[7] Unknown lady whose secret marriage is discussed in Boni, *Sordello*, p. xl.

[8] Many details of Sordel's life after he left Italy in

1228 are well-known. Before going to Provence
evidence suggests he spent some time in Spain and
(possibly) Portugal; in France he was supported by S.
de Mauleon, Blacatz, Barral des Baux, Raimon-Bérengar
IV and Charles of Anjou (Boni, *Sordello*, pp.
xlii-lii.)

[9] "Sweet Enemy." A *senhal* appearing in songs P.-C.
437.4a and 437.7, designating either Béatrice of Savoy
or Guida of Rodez.

95. TIBORS, NA

Lady Tibors[1] was a lady of Provence from a castle of
Lord Blacatz[2] which is called Seranon.[3] She was courtly
and learned, charming and extremely well informed. And she
knew how to invent poetry. And she loved well and was well
loved; and she was greatly honored by all the notable men in
that region, and greatly feared and greatly obeyed by all
the worthy ladies. And she composed these couplets and sent
them to her lover:

Fair handsome friend, I can tell you in truth
That I have never been without desire
Since I have know you and taken you as my
                                    lover.
And I have never been without desire
                        to see you often,
Fair handsome friend.
And I have never had occasion to regret.
Nor, if you left angry, have I ever
Had any joy until you returned.
And never...[4]

[1] Also Ticbors, Titbortz or Tibortz ("Tiburge").
[2] See Vida 21.
[3] Seranon is in the canton of Saint-Auban,

arrondissement of Grasse (Alpes-Maritimes).
[4] Bels dous amics, ben vos puosc en ver dir
Qe anc no fo q'eu estes ses desir,
Pos vos conuc [ni].us [pris] per fin aman;
Ni anc no fo q'eu non agues talan,
Bels douz amics, q'eu soven no.us veses,
Ni anc no fo sasons qe m'en pentis;
Ni anc no fo si vos n'anes iratz,
Q'eu agues joi, tro qe fosetz tornatz;
Ni anc ... (P.-C. 440.1)
See Schultz-Gora, p. 25 and Bogin, pp. 80-81.

96. TOMIER and PALAZI

Tomier and Lord Palazi[1] composed *sirventes* about the
King of Aragon[2] and about the counts of Provence[3] and of
Toulouse[4] and of the one from Baux,[5] and about tales which
circulated around Provence. And they were two knights from
Tarascon,[6] loved and cherished by the good knights and by
the ladies.

[1] Whether these two troubadours, authors of three
   sirventes, were brothers has been debated; see I.
   Frank, "Tomier e Palazi, troubadours tarasconnais",
   Romania, *78* (1957), 46-85, and Jeanroy, *Poésie
   lyrique*, I, 431.
[2] Jaime I (1208-1276).
[3] Raimon-Bérengar IV, count of Provence (d. 1245).
[4] Raimon VI of Toulouse (d. 1222) or Raimon VII of
   Toulouse.
[5] Guillem IV of Baux (d. 1218). See Vida 51.
[6] Seat of a canton in the arrondissement of Arles
   (Bouches-du-Rhône).

97. UC DE LA BACALARIA

Lord Uc de la Bacalaria[1] was from Limousin, from the same place as Gaucelm Faidit.[2] He was a minstrel of little merit, and he traveled little and was hardly known. And he composed good songs and composed a good *descort* and good *tensos*. And he was a courtly man, very capable and very learned.

[1] A town near Uzerche (Corrèze), now La Bachelerie. No edition exists of Uc's six poems; for the text of his collective dawn song, see J. Audiau, *Nouvelle anthologie des troubadours* (Paris, 1928), p. 91.
[2] See Vida 37.

98. UC BRUNET

Lord Uc Brunet[1] was from the city of Rodez,[2] which is in the suzerainty of the Count of Toulouse. And he was a cleric and was well versed in letters, and he was very clever at inventing poems and had a natural wit. And he became a minstrel and invented good songs, but he never composed melodies. And he frequented the King of Aragon[3] and the Count of Toulouse[4] and the Count of Rodez, his lord,[5] and Bernart d'Anduze[6] and the Dalfin d'Alvernhe.[7]

And he was in love with a burgher from Aurillac[8] whose name was my lady Galiana,[9] but she did not want to love or to keep him, nor give him any pleasure. And she took the Count of Rodez for her lover and dismissed Lord Uc Brunet. So Lord Uc Brunet, because of the pain he felt, entered the order of Cartosa.[10] And there he ended his days.

[1] Also Brunenc, Brunec. For discussion of this poet's name, see C. Brunel, "Les Troubadours Azemar Jordan et Uc Brunenc", *Romania*, *52* (1926), 505-508.

[2] Chief town of Aveyron.
[3] Probably Alfonso II, who died in 1196.
[4] Raimon VI, Count of Toulouse.
[5] Hugue II (1156-1195). See Chabaneau, *Biographies*, p. 243, note 3.
[6] Probably Bernard VII of Anduze, who died around 1223.
[7] See Vida 27.
[8] In the Basse-Auvergne, seat of the department of Cantal.
[9] The identity of this woman is not known.
[10] Unidentified Carthusian monastery.

99. UC DE MATAPLANA

[. . .][1] this news was heard throughout all these regions, far and near, and it came to be known of a worthy baron of Catalonia called Lord Uget de Mataplana.[2] He was a very clever and good inventor of poetry, and a very good friend of Miraval.[3] And he composed the *sirventes* which says:

I desire to compose a *sirventes*.[4]

[1] This text is a passage from a *razo* of Raimon de Miraval, found only in manuscript *H*. Uc was a favorite of King Pedro II of Aragon and a patron of troubadours (R. Vidal de Besalù among them).
[2] Uget is a diminutive of Uc. Mataplana is near Nuestra Señora de Mongrony in Ripoll, Spain.
[3] Raimon de Miraval, the troubadour; see Vida 87.
[4] D'un sirventes m'es pres talens (P.-C. 454.1).
See A. Caboni, "Le Poesie di Uc de Mataplana", *Cultura Neolatina*, *1* (1941), 216-221.

100. UC DE PENA

Ugo de Pena[1] was from Agenais[2] from a castle named
Monmessat, son of a merchant. And he became a minstrel and
sang well and knew a great number of songs composed by
others. And he knew very well the origins of the great men
of those regions. And he composed songs. He was a great
rogue, fond of gambling and staying in taverns. For this
reason he was always poor and without equipment. And he
went to the Isla e[n] Venaissi[3] in Provence to be wed.

[1] Pena is today Penne-d'Agenais in the arrondissement of
  Villeneuve-sur-Lot (Lot-et-Garonne).
[2] Region of Agen in Guyenne.
[3] Probably the Isle-sur-Sorgue, in the arrondissement of
  Avignon (Vaucluse).

101. UC DE SAINT CIRC

Lord Uc de Saint Circ was from Quercy,[1] from a town
named Thégra,[2] the son of a poor minor noble named Lord
Arman de Saint Circ because the castle from which he came is
called Saint Circ.[3] It is at the foot of Sainta-Maria de
Rocamadour,[4] which was destroyed and ruined by war. This
Uc had a great number of brothers older than he. And they
wanted to make him a cleric, and sent him to school in
Montpellier.[5] And while they thought that he was learning
letters, he learned songs and poems and *sirventes* and *tensos*
and couplets and the deeds and the sayings of the worthy men
and the worthy women who were living or had lived in the
world. And with this knowledge he became a minstrel.

And the Count of Rodez[6] and the Viscount of Turenne[7]
did much to elevate his stature among minstrels by the
tensos and the couplets they exchanged with him. And the
good Dauphin of Auvergne[8] did too.

And he spent a long time in Gascony, poor, sometimes on foot, sometimes on horseback. For a long time he was with the Countess of Benauges,[9] and through her he gained the friendship of Lord Savaric de Mauleon,[10] who provided him with equipment and with clothing. And he spent a long time with him in Poitou and in the neighboring regions, later in Catalonia and in Aragon and in Spain, with the good King Amfos[11] and with King Amfos de León[12] and with King Pedro of Aragon, and later in Provence with all the barons, then in Lombardy and in The Marche.[13] And he took a wife and had children.

He learned much from the knowledge of others, and he willingly passed it on to others. He composed very good songs and good melodies and good couplets. But he never accomplished much with songs,[14] for he was never really in love with any lady. But he knew well how to feign love to the ladies with his beautiful discourse. And he knew well how to express in his songs everything which happened to him because of them, and he knew well how to exalt them and how to belittle them. But after he took a wife, he never composed songs.

[1] Today the departments of Tarn-et-Garonne and Lot.
[2] Village in the canton of Gramat, not far from Rocamadour.
[3] Saint-Circ-d'Alzon, a village which no longer exists but is presumed to have been near Rocamadour, in the arrondissement of Gourdon (Lot).
[4] The manuscripts read *al pe de*. However, the castle could not have been built "at the foot" of the church, which is perched on a cliff overlooking the Alzon river valley. The church, Notre Dame de Rocamadour, has been a pilgrimage center since the Middle Ages. See A. Jeanroy and J. J. Salverda de Grave, *Poésies de Uc de Saint Circ* (Toulouse, 1913), pp. x, xi, and Boutière-Schutz, p. 242. See the latter volume for a critical edition of Uc's 44 poems.
[5] Seat of the department of Hérault.
[6] See Vida 25. Uc exchanged *coblas* and *partimens* with the Count of Rodez and probably served under him during the Albigensian Crusade.
[7] Probably Raimon III, who died in 1235 and was the brother of Maria de Ventadour. Uc exchanged two *tensos* with him.

[8] See Vida 27. Uc addressed a song to this poet, who was also a patron of troubadours.

[9] Guillerma de Benauges, a countess, was married to Peire de Gavarret, viscount of Benauges, a castle (now in ruins) in the commune of Arbis (Gironde).

[10] See Vida 93.

[11] Alfonso VIII of Castile (1158-1214).

[12] Alfonso IX of León (1187-1230).

[13] Of Treviso (*marca Trevisana*).

[14] The phrase *mas non fez gaires de las cansos* does not appear in manuscripts *AB*, and is accordingly discarded by Favati. Uc left over forty poems. It is understandable that his fifteen *cansos* (songs) could have been thought unimportant by the medieval biographer.

BRIEF GLOSSARY OF POETIC TERMS

Descort   Lyric composition featuring a different melody, rhyme and meter in each strophe, and expressing the poet's 'disagreement' or 'discord' with conventional poetic forms and themes.

Desplazens   Poem expressing 'dislike' or 'displeasure'.

Partimen (or *joc partit*)   Poem in the form of a debate in which the first speaker introduces a polemical issue or problem and chooses one of two possible solutions.   The second speaker rebutts.

Planh   A funeral lament, frequently enumerating the virtues and courtly qualities of the deceased, and expressing a sense of loss.

Razo   Prose commentary explaining the circumstances in which a poem was composed and often citing the particular verse passages it glosses.

Retroensa (or *retroncha*)   Isometric eight-syllable lyric which, like the estampie, is primarily a melodic composition.   Unlike estampies, *retroensas* have refrains.

Senhal   Secret name or code-name.

Sirventes   Moralizing poem, political, personal or didactic in tone, dealing with subjects other than love (war, politics, moral and social decadence of the time.)
Sirventes often imitate the melody and rhyme-scheme of love songs.

Tenso   Dialogue or debate poem in which two speakers express their points of view on one subject in alternating strophes of identical rhyme-schemes.

CHRONOLOGICAL LIST OF TROUBADOURS

EARLIEST TROUBADOURS

Guillem IX, Coms de Peitieus
Jaufre Rudel
Marcabru
Cercamon
Peire de Valeira
Peire Rogier
Richart de Berbezilh (Barbezieux)
Peire d'Alvernhe
Bernart de Ventadorn
Raimbaut d'Aurenga
Berengier de Palazol
Garin lo Brun

TROUBADOURS FROM THE LATE TWELFTH CENTURY

Azalais de Porcairagues
Giraut de Borneill (Bornelh)
Peire Bremon lo Tort
Guillem de Berguedan
Guilhem de Saint Leidier
Amfos d'Aragon
Raimon Jordan
Folquet de Marseilla
Arnaut Daniel
Raimon de Durfort and Turc Malec
Arnaut de Meruoill (Marueil)
Guiraudo lo Ros
Sail d'Escola
Bertran de Born
Gaucelm Faidit
Giraut de Salignac
La Comtessa de Dia
Almuc de Castelnou and Iseut de Capieu
Jordan Bonel
Peire de la Mula
Aimeric de Sarlat

Raimbaut de Vaqueiras
Peire Vidal
Guillem Magret
Peire Raimon de Toloza
Albert Marques

TROUBADOURS FROM THE EARLY THIRTEENTH CENTURY

Savaric de Mauleon
Rainaut and Jaufre de Pons
Bertran de Born the Younger
Perdigon
Aimeric de Peguilhan
Raimon de Miraval
Gui d'Uisel
Monge de Montaudon
Uc de la Bacalaria
Guillem de Cabestaing
Guiraut de Calanso
Uc de Mataplana
Raimon de las Salas
Guilhem Ademar
Peirol
Elias Cairel
Albertet
Tomier and Palazi
Pistoleta
Guillem de la Tor
Guillem Augier Novella
Uc Brunet
Maria de Ventadorn
Guillem de Balaun
Elias Fonsalada
Na Lombarda
Peire de Barjac
Ademar lo Negre
Guillem del Baus
Elias de Barjols
Gui de Cavaillon
Gausbert de Poicibot
Ricau de Tarascon
Folquet de Romans
Cadenet
Guillem Rainol d'At

Dalfi d'Alvernhe
Bertran del Pojet
Blacatz
Na Tibors
Pons de Capduoill
Guillem Figuera
Blacasset
Aimeric de Belenoi
Na Castelloza
Peire de Maensac

TROUBADOURS FROM THE MID-THIRTEENTH CENTURY

Uc de Saint Circ
Gauseran de Saint Leidier
Lanfranc Cigala
Lo coms de Rodes
Garin d'Apchier
Peire Guillem
Bertran d'Alamanon
Guillem de Montanhogol
Sordel
Peire Cardenal
Bertolome Zorzi
Daude de Pradas

TROUBADOURS FROM THE LATE THIRTEENTH CENTURY

Gausbert Amiel
Ferrari da Ferrara

TROUBADOURS OF UNCERTAIN DATE

Albertet Cailla
Peire de Bussignac
Uc de Pena

INDEX

123

For Product Safety Concerns and Information please contact our EU
representative GPSR@taylorandfrancis.com
Taylor & Francis Verlag GmbH, Kaufingerstraße 24, 80331 München, Germany